CONTENTS

POPULAR PRESS

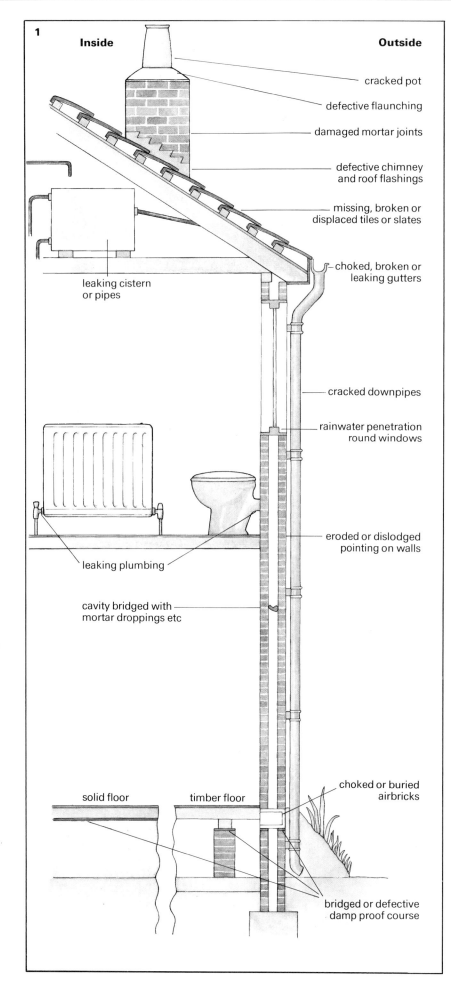

1 Inside   Outside

cracked pot

defective flaunching

damaged mortar joints

defective chimney
and roof flashings

missing, broken or
displaced tiles or slates

choked, broken or
leaking gutters

leaking cistern
or pipes

cracked downpipes

rainwater penetration
round windows

eroded or dislodged
pointing on walls

leaking plumbing

cavity bridged with
mortar droppings etc

solid floor   timber floor

choked or buried
airbricks

bridged or defective
damp proof course

Dealing with damp

Every house is prone to damp, both inside and out. Rain and snow batter the roof, walls, windows and doors, while moisture in the ground attacks the walls and floors from below. Inside the house, the plumbing pipework conveys water under floors and down walls as it travels to radiators, taps and tanks. To remain unaffected, a house must be structurally sound and well maintained; if it is not, damp will set in and bring plenty of problems with it.

The effects of damp may be manifested in relatively simple ways, such as wallpaper peeling off a wet wall or a wet patch appearing on a ceiling. In these cases, if prompt action is taken to cure the underlying cause of the problem, then all that remains to complete the repairs is a relatively straightforward decorating job. Where damp is allowed to remain untreated, more serious problems arise. There may be a dampish atmosphere throughout the house, mildew will form on clothes and a stale smell prevail. The occupants of the house may suffer ill health as a result of living in a constantly damp environment. Structural timbers such as floor joists and roof timbers may develop rot, making repair work complicated and expensive.

Protection against damp
Houses built in Britain since the 1920s are generally far less susceptible to damp than older properties since they have damp barriers incorporated into the structure which stop moisture working its way up through walls or floors (rising damp). In the concrete ground floor there is a damp proof membrane consisting of waterproof material stretched across the building from wall to wall to intercept moisture rising from the ground. The external cavity walls have a damp proof course laid in a mortar joint, usually between the second and third or third and fourth courses of bricks above ground level. This dpc, installed to prevent moisture creeping up the walls, is a strip of thin, impervious material, such as slate or bituminous felt, which stretches right round the external walls of the house to protect both the outer and inner leaves of brickwork.

Houses with suspended timber floors on the ground floor are generally far less prone to damp. Where there are problems, they are usually caused by a faulty dpc laid on the walls supporting the joists (sleeper walls) or by blocked up airbricks in the outside walls of the house. These bricks are designed to ensure a constant flow of air under the floor to keep the timber well ventilated and dry.

As well as rising damp there is also rainwater ingress or penetrating damp; this is prevented in modern houses by the air space in cavity walls. Rainwater which soaks through the outer leaf of bricks cannot cross the cavity and reach the inner

1 Faults in the house structure which can give rise to damp. Damage to chimney pots and the surrounding area should be repaired as soon as possible

leaf of bricks which form the outer walls of the rooms.

Faults in damp proofing Assuming the roof and gutters etc. of the house are sound, a modern house should remain free of damp. But problems may arise if faulty damp proof materials are used or errors occur at the building stage. For example, a split in a floor membrane or wall dpc will allow moisture through; and if mortar is allowed to fall into the cavity during building it could land on and set across one of the metal ties linking the walls to form a perfect bridge for moisture to cross over to the inner leaf of the wall.

Older houses Where there are no purpose-made damp proof barriers incorporated in the structure, the thickness of the materials used may prevent moisture creeping right through solid walls and floors. The density of some of these materials means moisture takes a long time to soak in and will dry out in settled weather without damp ever showing inside the house. On the other hand, with walls made of very porous material, moisture may well soak right through and, in severe weather conditions, tell-tale wet patches appear on interior surfaces.

Damp or condensation?

While damp is easily confused with condensation, since both produce similar wet stains on walls, it is important to differentiate between the two since remedial treatments vary. Condensation is readily recognized when it causes misting on windows or beads of moisture to drip from water pipes or the WC cistern; identification problems arise when a wet stain shows on other surfaces. Usually the weather will pin-point the problem; on a wet muggy day or during periods of prolonged rain, wet stains indicate rising damp or rainwater ingress. On a cold, dry day wet stains on walls, especially when accompanied by the more familiar signs of misty windows etc, point to condensation.

Checking for damp

Normally any wet patches caused by damp which appear inside the house can be linked to a structural fault nearby. For example, a wet patch high up on an upstairs wall could be the result of a leaking gutter or downpipe and one at skirting board level on the ground floor is probably caused by a defective or non-existent dpc. Random patches on walls point to rainwater ingress, while wet stains on ceilings could be traced back to a cracked roof tile or leaking plumbing.

Chimney stack Damp appearing on chimney-breast walls can indicate rainwater ingress in the chimney stack area. This problem is often created or accentuated by blocking off the air supply to the flue after removing a fireplace. A broken or loose chimney pot may need to be removed or replaced; if the flue is no longer used, you can fix a special capping pot which allows for ventilation but keeps out rainwater. Other common faults in chimneys are cracked flaunching (the sloping layer of mortar securing the pot), crumbling mortar joints between the brickwork of the stack, which should be re-pointed, and defective or loose flashings (the materials, usually zinc or lead, which seal the joint between the base of the stack and the roof). These can be stepped, with one edge secured in rising mortar courses of the chimney stack brickwork, or a straight band around the base of the stack, known as apron flashing.

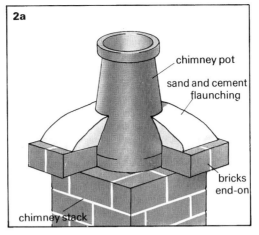

2a If damp appears on chimney-breast walls, check the condition of the chimney pots, flaunching and the chimney stack
2b Check also the flashings round the chimney stack are sound and there are no loose or missing tiles or slates

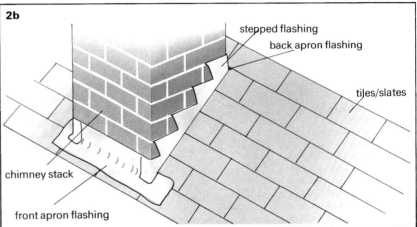

Roof Slipped or missing tiles or slates will admit rainwater to the felt beneath, which will sag, eventually split and allow water to drip onto the loft floor and show on the ceiling of the room below. Loft timbers kept constantly wet by dripping water will rot quickly so you should replace the missing roof covering as soon as possible. Fine cracks in tiles or slates will allow rainwater to seep inside; it may be difficult to spot cracks from the ground and the best way to find them is to climb into the loft during heavy rainfall and look and listen for drips. You can then trace these back to their source which could be some way from the dripping water.

Gutters and downpipes Where the rainwater drainage system is working properly, water falling off the roof is collected in the gutters from where it flows steadily into the downpipe to be discharged to the drain below. If the system fails, a large volume of water may drain onto one area of a wall, causing the brickwork to absorb an excessive amount of moisture.

Walls Where a wall has a solid covering of rendering, roughcast or pebbledash and is kept well painted with a good quality exterior paint, damp problems from rainwater ingress should never arise. However, if the wall covering is cracked or loose and the mortar joints in the brickwork behind are in poor shape or there is no decorative paint finish, then rainwater can soak through.

Treating damp

Plain unpainted solid brick walls rely completely on the density of the material and sound mortar joints to keep out rain, so any loose or crumbling joints should be repointed. If walls are in good

3a Installing a damp proof course using the liquid method is a job you can tackle yourself — as long as you are prepared for the large amount of work involved
3b With the strip method, the dpc is inserted in slots cut in the mortar with a power saw
3c Electro osmosis treatment involves inserting electrodes in the wall and linking them through a copper strip; this is connected to a terminal buried in the ground
3d With the capillary method, porous ceramic tubes are set into the wall

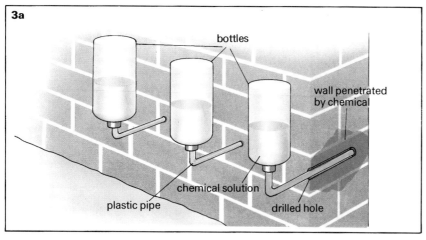

3a

bottles

wall penetrated by chemical

chemical solution

plastic pipe

drilled hole

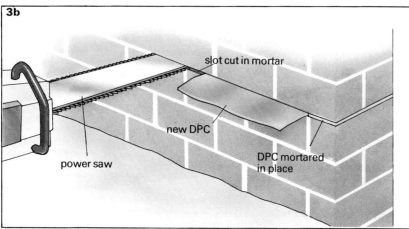

3b

slot cut in mortar

new DPC

power saw

DPC mortared in place

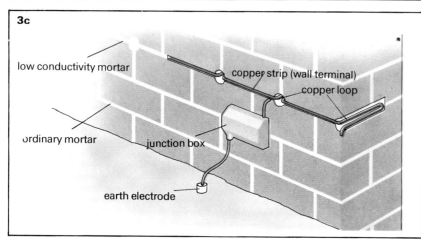

3c

low conductivity mortar

copper strip (wall terminal)

copper loop

ordinary mortar

junction box

earth electrode

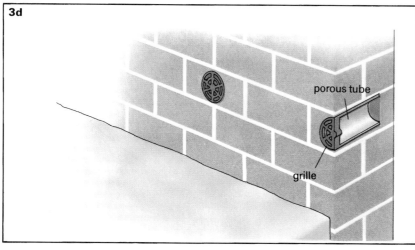

3d

porous tube

grille

repair but damp shows inside, a brush coating of a silicone water repellent liquid applied to the outside of the house should cure the trouble. These colourless liquids keep out the rain but still allow moisture vapour trapped in the wall to escape. There are also liquid treatments for internal application; but these are simply sealers which prevent moisture from affecting decorative materials and are not intended to cure the damp problem. Similarly, you can apply a dry lining to walls using materials such as bitumen-backed aluminium foil or steel corrugated sheets before decorating, but again these do not cure the damp itself.

Rising damp in walls can be treated by one of four methods of installing a dpc. With one exception they are probably best left to a specialist.

Liquid treatment A chemical liquid is fed into the wall and diffuses through the brickwork to form a damp proof barrier. The liquid can be injected under pressure using special equipment or be left to soak into the wall from a number of special bottles located in a series of pre-drilled holes. This treatment is one you can carry out yourself and will be covered in greater detail later.

Dpc strip method A power saw is used to cut through a mortar course right round the outside of walls and a damp proof material such as lead, copper or polythene is slipped into the saw cut. (Slate is not normally used since saws generally do not cut a wide enough slot for this material and laborious chipping out is needed.) Fresh mortar is then inserted to complete the process.

Electro-osmosis The difference in the electrical charge between the wall and the ground causes damp to rise in the wall. The electro-osmosis system involves fitting electrodes into the wall and linking them through a copper strip which is, in turn, linked to an electrode driven into the ground. Minute electric charges in a wet wall are then discharged down the link to prevent moisture rising.

Capillary Holes are drilled into the walls, either from the inside or outside of the house, and porous ceramic tubes inserted; these are bonded into the holes with special porous mortar and then fitted with a protective evaporation cap. Moisture from the brickwork or plaster is drawn through the pores in the tube and then evaporates into the air. The installation of this process involves the minimum amount of disturbance to the structure.

Warning Before going to the trouble and expense of installing a new dpc, check that something more basic is not causing the trouble. The existing dpc may be perfectly sound but could have been bypassed by earth or a rockery piled against the wall. Paths beside a wall should be 150mm (6in) below dpc level or rainwater will constantly splash above the dpc; in times of torrential rain, water on the path could soak the wall above dpc level.

Solid floors Normally a suitable damp proof barrier can be applied by brushing or trowelling on a damp-proofing liquid such as pitch epoxy sealer or rubberized bituminous emulsion, though sometimes a plastic membrane sheet can be used instead. Remove the skirtings temporarily and take the damp proofing material up the wall to link with the wall dpc. Where the problem is more acute, a sandwich treatment is required. Apply two coats of damp proofing material, allowing the first to dry before applying the second. Sprinkle some clean, sharp sand over the second coat while it is still tacky to form a key for a finishing screed 50mm (2in) thick.

Repointing bricks

Good quality brickwork is generally a maintenance-free structural material; but as a building ages the exposed surfaces of the mortar joints may show signs of decay and need repointing. There are a number of reasons why this may happen.

Poor mix The original mortar mix may have been of incorrect proportions.

Moisture Driving rains, a faulty damp proof course or leaking gutters and downpipes may have allowed water to penetrate the mortar.

Frosts Any moisture in the mortar or bricks will freeze, expand and break up the surface if subjected to heavy frosts.

Pollution In heavy industrial areas, sulphates in the atmosphere will cause deterioration.

Structural movement Inadequate foundations or a poor standard of building will break up the stability of the mortar.

Where the cause of mortar failure can be diagnosed, it should be remedied, if possible, before repointing, which itself should not be carried out during cold weather because of the possibility of frost affecting the new mortar before it has dried. If winter working is unavoidable, you must use plenty of waterproof sheeting to keep off icy winds, rain and frosts.

1 Raking out old mortar. **2** Repointing tools: cold chisel for removing old mortar **(top)**; plugging chisel, with groove same width as mortar, ideal for raking out **(centre)**; frenchman made by bending end of old kitchen knife **(bottom)**

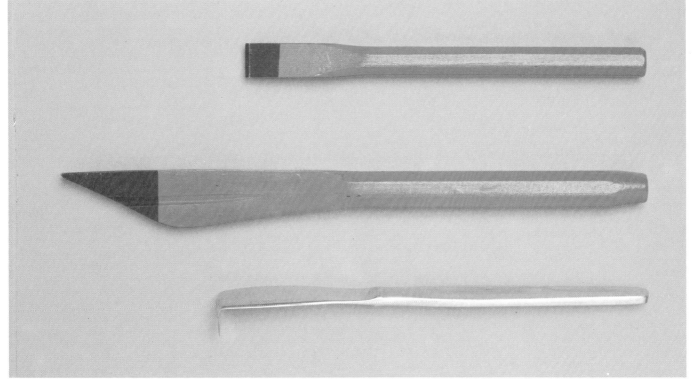

How to repoint

You should always start repointing at the top of the brickwork and work downwards, covering about two square metres (21sq ft) at a time. Scrape any moss or lichen from the surface and then rake out mortar joints to a depth of about 15mm (or ½in), taking care not to damage the brickwork. The recess must be left square (otherwise the mortar may fall out); this can be done with a cold chisel or with a tool you make yourself by filing one end of a square section length of steel. After raking out, ensure the brick edges are free from old mortar and brush out all traces of dust with a fibre bristle brush.

Dry brickwork should be dampened, not soaked, with clean water before repointing; this is important in hot weather when bricks store heat. Water will reduce any suction from the old mortar and brickwork, but too much on the surface could cause the freshly applied mortar to run down the face of the bricks. An old distemper brush is ideal for dampening.

What mix to use

The mortar should be chosen carefully to suit the existing brickwork and the amount of exposure it is likely to undergo. A general mix, suitable for most brickwork, consists of one part cement, one part lime and six parts of washed builder's sand. For a soft facing brick a mix of one part cement, two parts lime and nine parts sand would be satisfactory. Where hard, dense bricks are used in situations of extreme exposure a mix of one part cement, a quarter part lime and three parts sand should be used. This richer cement mix is more likely to

3 Brushing away dust after raking out mortar. **4** Dampening brickwork with distemper brush. **5** Applying mortar with pointing trowel. **6** Forming weathered joint with frenchman and timber straight-edge. **7** Mortar levelled with face of bricks above and below. **8** Making rounded or tooled joint. **9** Forming recessed joint with square timber

7

8

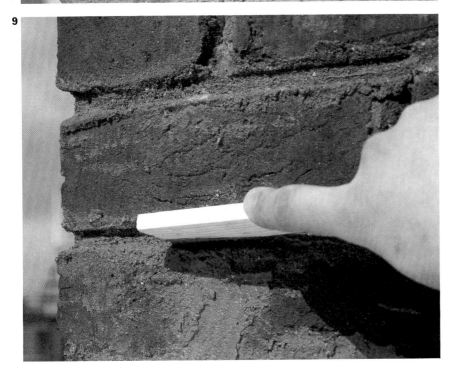

9

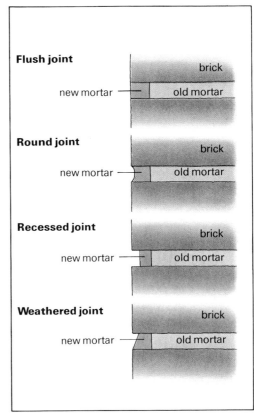

Flush joint

brick

new mortar — old mortar

Round joint

brick

new mortar — old mortar

Recessed joint

brick

new mortar — old mortar

Weathered joint

brick

new mortar — old mortar

shrink and there is a possibility of hairline cracks forming between the bricks and mortar.

As each batch is used, the joints already filled should be tooled or cut and loose material brushed away. When the colour of mortar is important, a ready-mixed coloured mix should be used to maintain consistency.

Warning Make small amounts of mortar at a time and discard it as soon as it begins to dry.

Types of pointing

Different pointing effects can be employed, depending on the type of brickwork and the style of joint used when the house was built.

Weathered The most effective way of shedding rain away from the bricks. Apply the mortar firmly with a small pointing trowel. Push the blade edge at the top of the joint to form a slight recess that slopes forward to meet the top edge of the brick below. You can form this angle using a straight-edge with the edge of the trowel or use a small tool called a 'frenchman' together with the straight-edge; this tool can easily be made by bending the end of a long thin kitchen knife.

Flush Usually employed when matching old brickwork, it is formed by applying the new mortar level with the face of the bricks above and below.

Round or tooled joint A variation on a flush joint, it is also used mainly when matching old brickwork. First form the flush joint and then run a thin rounded piece of timber along the mortar face.

Recessed joint Used solely when matching existing recessed joints in brickwork. After forming a flush joint, the recess is raked back by using a square section piece of timber of the exact width of the mortar joint.

Having finished pointing, remember to remove carefully any remaining deposits of mortar from the face of the brickwork – before the mortar is thoroughly dry – with a fibre bristle brush.

Repairing external window sills

Timber window sills

Flaking paintwork is one of the first signs of rotting wood, but even an outwardly sound paint surface can, on closer inspection, be hiding a multitude of troubles. If you suspect rot in a sill strip off the paint and cut back any rotting areas until you reach sound timber. If the exposed timber looks grey it is suffering from surface decay, which you must skim away before repainting. When removing affected areas take out any nails or screws in the surface and plane down until you reach clean, healthy timber.

Don't forget to check the underside of the sill as well. Dig a sharp penknife into the wood; if it goes in easily these soft parts will have to be dug out and stripped back as before.

An important part of the sill is the drip groove, a U-shaped channel running the length of the underside. This ensures a free passage for rainwater and must therefore be kept free of dirt.

If you have discovered rot in its early stages you will have only small cavities to fill. This operation is carried out using a hard stopping such as an exterior wood filler or waterproof stopping.
Warning If you use putty instead of a hard stopping, when the sill has been repainted the oil content trapped beneath the surface of paint film could cause blistering when the paint is subjected to excessive heat.

Let the stopping set according to the manufacturer's instructions and sand smooth. Where resinous (sticky) knots are revealed apply a coat of shellac knotting and leave to dry before painting. Repaint the entire surface with primer, undercoat and top coat.

Where it has been necessary to remove a large chunk of rotten timber, to repair by filling would not only be impractical but unsound. Here you will need to make good by cutting a new piece of timber with a panel saw to the same size as that removed. Position the new piece of timber and mark a drip groove in pencil, following the line of the existing groove. Remove and tenon saw the groove to the required depth and width, gouging out the waste timber with a narrow chisel. Glasspaper smooth for a clean finish.

Fix the new piece of timber in position with exterior adhesive and galvanized nails. Sink the nail heads below the surface with a nail punch and fill the cavities with exterior filler or waterproof stopping. Repaint as before.

The most troublesome timber is oak which, because of its open grain, tends to encourage breakdown of the paint. Here strip back to bare wood and rub fine surface filler well down into the grain with a piece of clean rag. Let it set and then smooth with glasspaper, working only with the grain. Finally apply a coat of aluminium primer, then undercoat and top coats of paint.

Ideally oak is best left in its natural state and protected by coating with boiled linseed oil or a timber preservative. So when you strip the sill decide which finish you want – natural or painted.

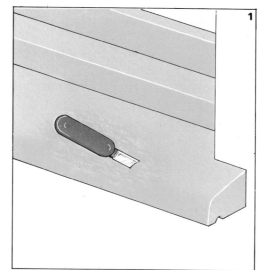

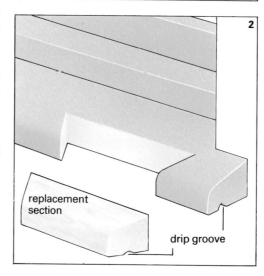

replacement section

drip groove

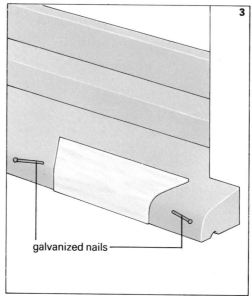

galvanized nails

1 Checking for decay in timber window sill with sharp knife
2 Extensive rot removed and new piece of timber cut to fit gap with drip groove to match existing one
3 New timber fixed into place with exterior adhesive and galvanized nails

Overleaf
4 Badly rotted timber sill cut away to be replaced with new one cast in concrete
5a Timber shuttering box supported on batten screwed to wall below window frame. Sash cord stretched along base of box and knotted through holes in box ends gives line of drip groove (see 6)
5b Cast concrete sill is smoothed level to top edges of timbers with steel float
6 Detail of drip groove at side of sill, with knotted cord in place. Remove cord when concrete is set

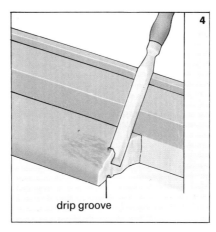
Making a concrete sill

In extreme cases of rotting, where the sill has to be removed completely, it is worth casting a new one of your own in concrete. This is not difficult or expensive and removes forever the possibility of rot.

Chisel out all remaining pieces of the old sill. Apply one coat of acrylic primer to the bare wood of the frame for protection and apply a second coat immediately prior to casting the sill. To reinforce the concrete, drive a row of 150mm (6in) nails, 150mm apart and a third of their length, into the timber along the bottom of the window frame.

You must then construct a shuttering box from 25mm (1in) thick timber, screwed together, into which you pour the concrete. The tops of the sides of the box should slope slightly downwards away from the wall to prevent rainwater from collecting on the sill and causing possible rotting of the window frame. To support the shuttering box screw a batten to the wall below the window frame, ensuring the screws are well anchored. Remember to make the top of the box the level you intend as the top surface of the sill, and that the inside measurements of the box will be the outside measurements of the sill.

For your drip groove, stretch a length of stout cord – sashcord is ideal – along the base of the box and through specially drilled holes in the side pieces, knotting at both ends to keep it taut.

Mixing the concrete

Using one part fine shingle, two parts clean sharp sand and one part cement, add water gradually until you have a buttery, rather than sloppy, consistency. Shovel the mix into the shuttering box and smooth level with the top edges of the timbers with a steel float. Care will be needed to maintain an even downward slope in the centre of the new sill. Before you remove the box frame, cord and wall batten, allow a few days for the concrete to set thoroughly. The job is completed by painting with a proprietary concrete paint.

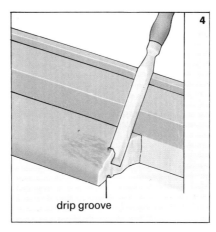

4
drip groove

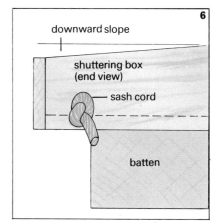

6
downward slope
shuttering box
(end view)
sash cord
batten

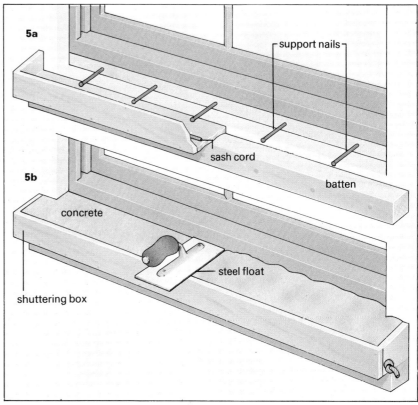

5a
support nails
sash cord
batten

5b
concrete
steel float
shuttering box

Types of roof tile

Before attempting repairs to a tiled roof, you need to know what sort of tiles have been used and how they are laid out on the roof. Tiles are made of either clay or concrete, with a variety of designs to choose from.

Types of concrete tile: **1** Bonnet hip; **2** Valley; **3** 90 degree angle – right; **4** 90 degree angle – left; **5** Baby ridge; **6** Ridge; **7** Tile-and-a-half tiles; **8** Plain tiles; **9 & 10** Plain tiles with arrowhead and bullnose; **11** Modern interlocking; **12** Bold roll interlocking; **13** Wessex interlocking; **14** Plastic rooflight; **15** Ludlow Major interlocking; **16** Mendip interlocking **Opposite page 1** English pantiles. **2** Single Roman. **3** Double Roman. **4** Spanish. **5** Italian. **6** Interlocking Somerset. **7** Interlocking concrete. **8** Interlocking vertical joint concrete. **9** Monopitch ridge. **10** Rooflight

There are specially shaped tiles designed for use on specific areas of the roof, but there are basically two types of roofing tile – double lap (or plain), and single lap.

Double lap tiles

Double lap, or plain, tiles are slightly curved with two holes for fixing nails and usually two nibs, or projections, on the underside at the top edge; some tiles, however, are continuously nibbed along the top edge. The tiles are normally fixed to battens with aluminium alloy nails and the nibs hook over the battens for extra security. The camber, or curve, to each tile provides air spaces between tiles and battens for ventilation and to prevent water ingress by capillary action.

Once made by hand, plain tiles are now mainly machine-made from clay or concrete. Many clay tiles are smooth-faced, although they are also available with a sand face. Concrete tiles are becoming increasingly popular because they are slightly cheaper than many clay tiles; they are also not so likely to laminate (or flake) and are available in a wide range of colours, including brown, red, grey, green and buff. In some cases the colour is confined to the granule facing, although often the tiles are coloured throughout. Because there are many types, sizes and colours of plain tiles, take a sample as a pattern when ordering replacements to make sure you get the right ones.

In plain tiling, the tiles hook over roofing battens so each course overlaps the tiles in the course-but-one below it; this amount of overlap (called the lap) should not be less than 65mm (2½in). Tiles in each course are butted together side by side and do not overlap. In this way there are at least two thicknesses of tile in every part of the roof – and three thicknesses in most places.

The usual size of plain tiles is 265 × 165mm (10½ × 6½in), although some hand-made tiles are 280 × 178mm (11 × 7in). In addition there are special tiles to maintain the lap and weatherproof the roof at the verge (the side of the roof), eaves (gutter level) and ridge (the apex of the roof).

Verge tiles At the verges special tile-and-a-half tiles, usually 265 × 248mm (10½ × 9¾in), are used in alternate courses. These tiles are normally bedded on an undercloak of plain tiles, laid face downwards and projecting 38–50mm (1½–2in) over the gable walls or bargeboards. Sometimes the verge is finished with a clip-on plastic verge channel which holds the end tiles firmly and stops water penetration.

Eaves tiles These usually measure 190 × 165mm (7½ × 6½in) and are used as an undercourse at the eaves and as a top course just below the ridge tiles.

Ridge tiles Half-round ridge tiles, bedded with mortar along their edges and at the joints between tiles, are used to weatherproof the ridge. Hog back, segmental (or third-round) and angle ridge tiles are also used. It is most important the bedding mortar is placed only along the edges and joints between the ridge tiles, since cracking can occur if the ridge tiles are filled with bedding mortar.

Hip tiles There are several ways in which hips (the junction of two sides of the roof) may be finished. It is common to use third-round ridge tiles bedded on mortar in a similar fashion to the way a ridge is formed. Because third-round tiles are not secured by nailing, a galvanized hip iron is screwed to the foot of the hip rafter before the hip tiles are laid to give them support.

Hip irons are not necessary when bonnet hip or angular hip tiles are used. These are nailed to the hip rafter and are bedded on mortar at the tail; they should be fitted so they lie snugly against the plain tiling at each side.

Valley tiles In plain tiling, valleys are often formed with purpose-made valley tiles of similar colour and texture to the main roof tiles. Valley tiles butt against plain tiles on each side and are usually fixed by nailing or bedding in mortar.

Single lap tiles

Single lap tiles are designed to overlap, or be overlapped by, adjacent tiles in the same course and in the course above and below. In most parts of the roof there is only a single thickness of tile – except at overlaps, when there is a double thickness.

Clay single lap tiles have been in use for many years, but are being replaced by interlocking concrete tiles which are cheaper. Although some clay patterns are still made, it may be difficult to buy replacements; if they are not stocked by your local builders' merchant, try specialist roofing contractors or local demolition firms – but ensure second hand tiles are not flaking or cracking.

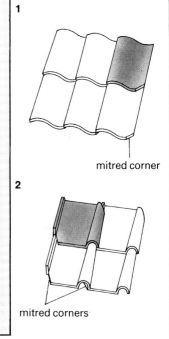

1

mitred corner

2

mitred corners

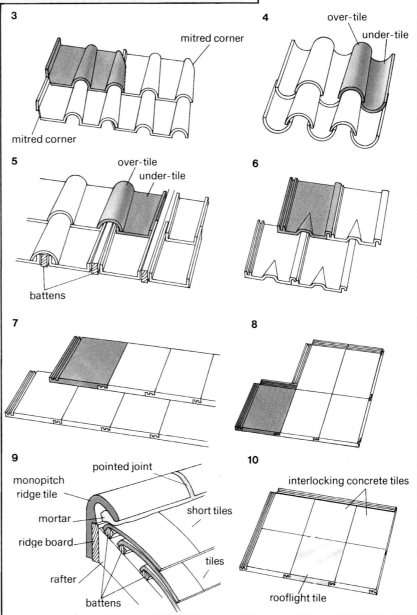

3

mitred corner

mitred corner

4

over-tile

under-tile

5

over-tile

under-tile

battens

6

7

8

9

monopitch ridge tile

pointed joint

mortar

short tiles

ridge board

rafter

tiles

battens

10

interlocking concrete tiles

rooflight tile

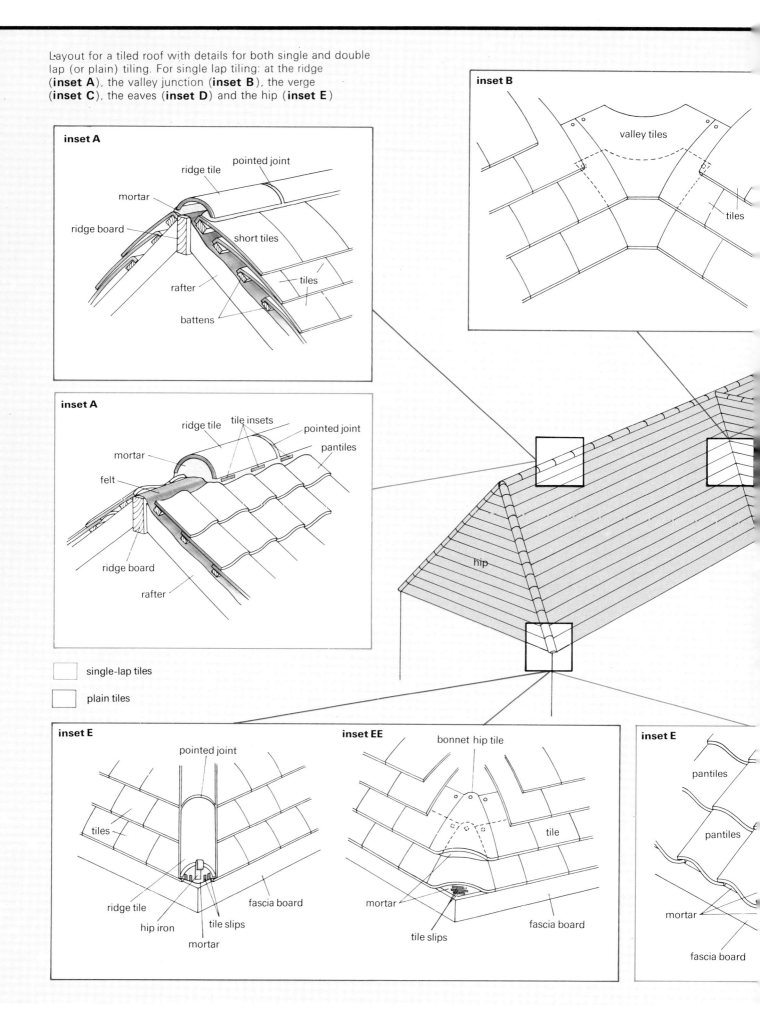

Layout for a tiled roof with details for both single and double lap (or plain) tiling. For single lap tiling: at the ridge (**inset A**), the valley junction (**inset B**), the verge (**inset C**), the eaves (**inset D**) and the hip (**inset E**)

inset A

pointed joint

ridge tile

mortar

ridge board

short tiles

rafter

tiles

battens

inset A

ridge tile

tile insets

pointed joint

pantiles

mortar

felt

ridge board

rafter

single-lap tiles

plain tiles

inset B

valley tiles

tiles

hip

inset E

pointed joint

tiles

ridge tile

hip iron

tile slips

mortar

fascia board

inset EE

bonnet hip tile

tile

mortar

tile slips

fascia board

inset E

pantiles

pantiles

mortar

fascia board

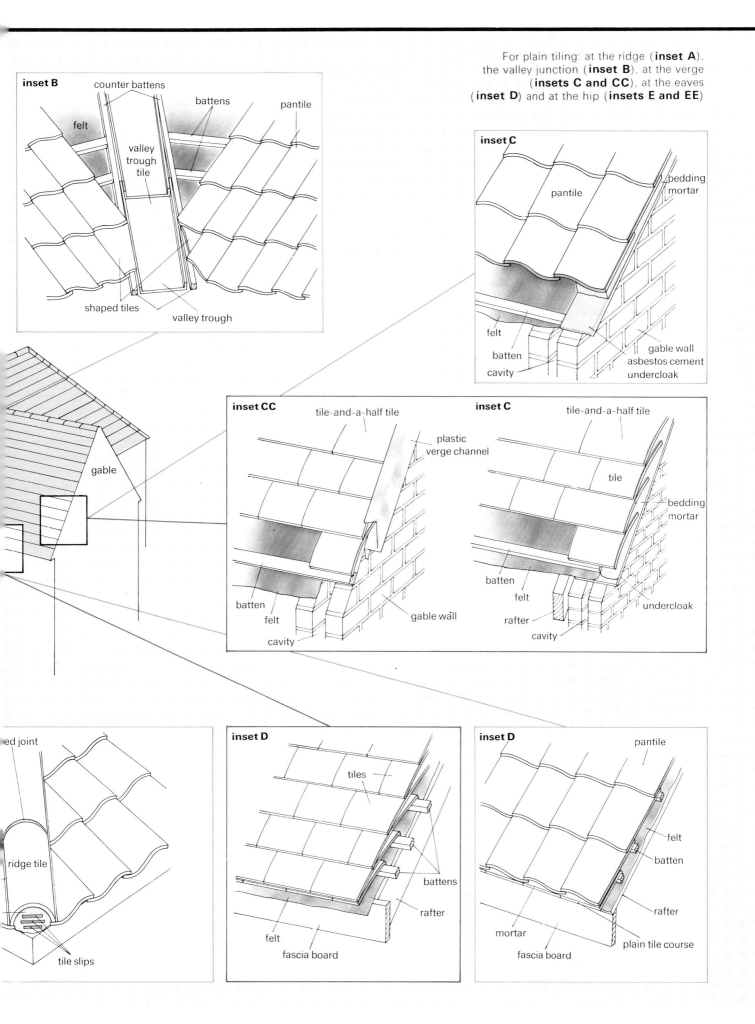

For plain tiling: at the ridge (**inset A**), the valley junction (**inset B**), at the verge (**insets C and CC**), at the eaves (**inset D**) and at the hip (**insets E and EE**)

inset B

counter battens

battens

pantile

felt

valley trough tile

shaped tiles

valley trough

inset C

pantile

bedding mortar

felt

batten

cavity

gable wall asbestos cement undercloak

gable

inset CC

tile-and-a-half tile

plastic verge channel

batten

felt

cavity

gable wall

inset C

tile-and-a-half tile

tile

bedding mortar

batten

felt

rafter

cavity

undercloak

ed joint

ridge tile

tile slips

inset D

tiles

battens

rafter

felt

fascia board

inset D

pantile

felt

batten

rafter

mortar

fascia board

plain tile course

15

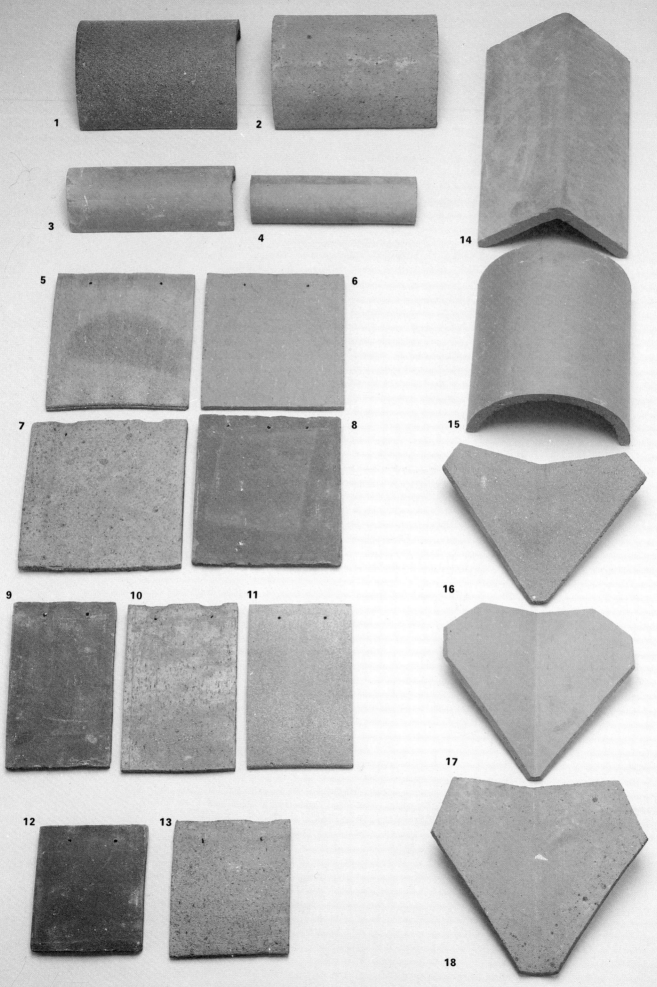

1

2

3

4

5

6

7

8

9

10

11

12

13

14

15

16

17

18

16

A selection of some of the many types of clay tile available; it should help you to recognize the tiles on your roof. Try builders' merchants for replacements; they should be able to order tiles for you if they do not have them in stock

1 Hawkins half-round ridge
2 Dreadnought half-round ridge
3 Half-round baby ridge
4 Pascall roll ridge
5 Hawkins machine-made tile-and-a-half
6 Rosemary machine-made tile-and-a-half
7 Dreadnought hand-made tile-and-a-half
8 Keymer hand-made tile-and-a-half
9 Keymer 265 × 165mm hand-made and sand-faced
10 Dreadnought 280 × 178mm hand-made
11 Hawkins 265 × 165mm machine-made, sand-faced
12 Keymer hand-made eaves
13 Dreadnought hand-made eaves
14 Angle ridge
15 Round ridge
16 Hawkins machine-made valley
17 Rosemary machine-made valley
18 Dreadnought hand-made valley
19 Six patterns of interlocking tiles, glazed and unglazed
20 Dreadnought machine-made bonnet hip
21 Rosemary machine-made bonnet hip
22 Rosemary machine-made arris hip
23 Rosemary machine-made 90 degree angle

A commonly found single lap tile is the English pantile; you can also buy interlocking clay pantiles which are available in a range of colours and with a glazed or matt finish. In some situations only alternate pantiles are nailed to the roofing battens but, if you have to replace this type of tile, it is a good idea to fix each one with rustless aluminium alloy nails (you may have to drill fixing holes at the top of the tiles using a masonry drill bit).

Other common single lap clay tiles are double and single Roman tiles, interlocking Somerset tiles, Spanish tiles which have concave under-tiles, and Italian tiles which have flat under-tiles.

Interlocking concrete tiles are available in a wide range of designs and colours and in smooth and granule finishes. Some have an acrylic finish which gives the roof a lustre as well as promoting rainflow off the roof and inhibiting the growth of fungi and moss. Concrete tiles imitate many of the clay tile designs and some are patterned to look like roofing slates.

Some single lap tiles have interlocking head and tail joints as well as interlocking side joints; this enables them to be used on roofs with very low pitches (or slopes) – down to 15 degrees in some cases. (Compare this with the minimum pitch for a plain roof tile which is 35 degrees.)

Fittings Fittings for use with interlocking concrete tiles include angle, half-round and third-round ridge tiles, as well as monopitch ridge tiles for monopitch roofs.

Rooflight tiles To give light in the roof space, rooflight tiles made from translucent reinforced plastic are available in the contours of the single lap roof tile patterns.

Valley trough tiles Valleys can be formed with special valley trough tiles, with adjacent tiles neatly cut and bedded on mortar.

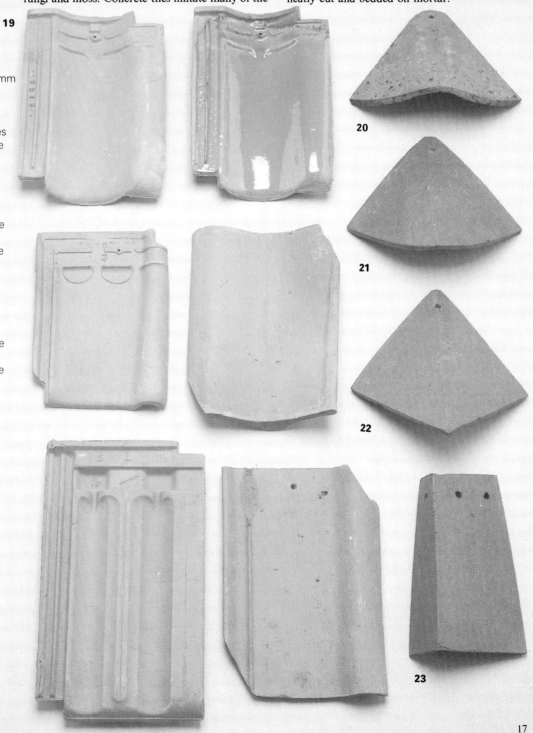

19

20

21

22

23

Repairing a tiled roof

While most roof repair jobs are easy and straight-forward, difficulties arise because the work has to be done at height; this may well deter some people from tackling them. Make safety the number one priority: whenever possible use a scaffold tower to reach the roof and to give a working platform at gutter level; always use roof crawling boards to enable you to climb on the roof.

Double lap (plain) tiles Any remaining parts of broken or crumbling plain tiles must be removed before new tiles can be fitted. To release the tile-holding nibs from the roofing battens, use small pieces of timber to lift up the tiles in the course above the tiles to be replaced; then lift the broken tile over the batten with a bricklayer's trowel. If the tile is held by nails, it may be possible to work it loose by moving the tile from side to side while prising up the tile with the tip of a trowel. Should this method fail, use a slate ripper to cut the heads off the nails; hook the blade of the ripper round the nail and pull to cut through it. Normally only the tiles in every fourth course are nailed, but in particularly exposed positions all the tiles may be nailed to prevent them being lifted by the wind.

Fit the replacement tile under the tiles in the row above, pushing it upwards until the nibs hook over the batten. Again, a trowel under the tile will help you to position it accurately. A tile without nibs can be held in place with a gap-filling adhesive applied from a special gun.

Single lap tiles These are fairly easily displaced, so where possible fix each tile with one or two 32mm (1¼in) aluminium alloy nails into the roofing batten or secure the tile with a clip nailed onto the batten, where this system is used on your roof.

Clay pantiles This type is often simply hung on battens. If they become dislodged, it is best to drill holes at the top of the tiles, using a masonry drill bit, and refix them with aluminium alloy nails.

Ridge tiles If the joints between ridge tiles have cracked but the tiles themselves are still firmly bedded, you can repair the joints with beads of non-hardening mastic applied with a mastic gun, or with thick bitumen mastic trowelled into the joints.

Loose ridge tiles must be lifted and rebedded on a mortar mix of one part Portland cement to four parts sharp, washed sand. Soak the tiles in water and place the mortar along the edges of the tiles

Above Replacing ridge tiles on a roof: always handle the tiles with care and remember they are much heavier than they look

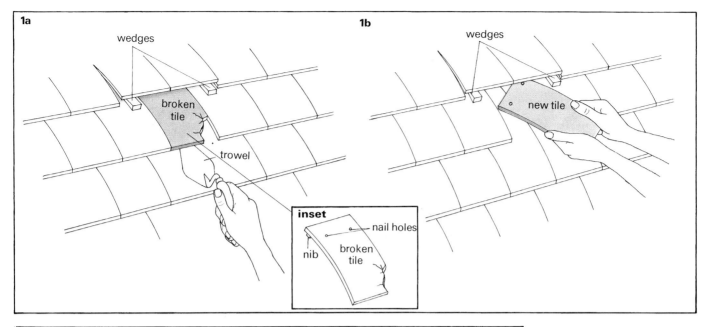

1a | **1b**

wedges | wedges

broken tile | new tile

trowel

inset

nail holes

nib | broken tile

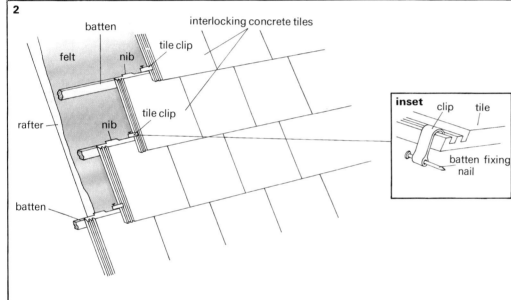

2

batten

interlocking concrete tiles

felt | tile clip | nib

rafter | tile clip | nib

batten

inset | clip | tile

batten fixing nail

1a To remove a damaged tile, use timber wedges to raise the tiles in the row above and lift the tile with a trowel until the holding nibs are clear of the roofing batten

1b Fit the replacement tile under the tiles in the row above, pushing it up until the nibs hook over the roofing batten

2 Some single lap interlocking tiles are held in place with clips; the clip hooks over the tile and is nailed to the batten (**inset**)

3 To repair cracked joints between ridge tiles, rake out the old mortar and replace it with beads of non-hardening mastic applied from a mastic gun

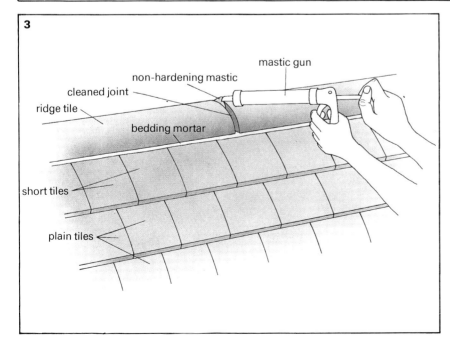

3

mastic gun

non-hardening mastic

cleaned joint

ridge tile

bedding mortar

short tiles

plain tiles

and at the joints. It is important not to fill the tiles completely with mortar because the cavity allows air to circulate under the tiles, helping them to dry out quickly after rainfall and reducing cracking.

To close the cavity at each end of the ridge, use flat pieces of tile (called tile slips) set in mortar – any pieces of scrap tile will serve this purpose.

Hip tiles These are usually bedded on mortar in the same way as ridge tiles; repairs are the same as for ridge tiles except hips are usually prevented from slipping down the roof by a hip iron. If this has corroded, it should be replaced; new galvanized hip irons are obtainable from builders' merchants. Carefully lift the hip tile adjacent to the hip iron, remove the old bedding mortar and the remains of the hip iron. Screw the new iron to the foot of the hip rafter using rustproof screws and rebed the hip tiles on cement mortar, filling the open end with small pieces of tile set in mortar.

Bonnet hip tiles are fixed at the top with aluminium alloy nails, while the tail (exposed part) is bedded on cement mortar. If only one bonnet hip tile has to be replaced, it may be possible to fix it without disturbing the other hip tiles by using a

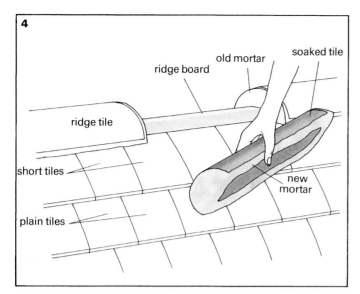

4

ridge board
old mortar
soaked tile
ridge tile
short tiles
plain tiles
new mortar

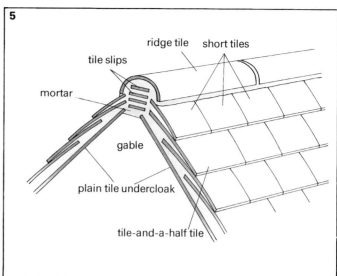

5

ridge tile
short tiles
tile slips
mortar
gable
plain tile undercloak
tile-and-a-half tile

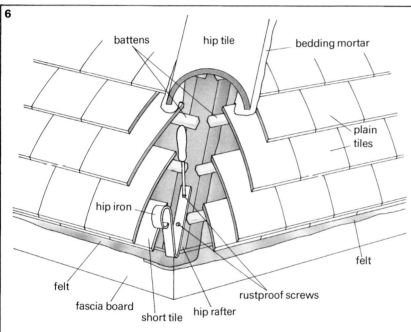

6

battens
hip tile
bedding mortar
plain tiles
hip iron
felt
felt
fascia board
rustproof screws
short tile
hip rafter

mortar mix of one part fine sand to one part cement. If you cannot do this, you will have to strip off all the tiles and renail them, working from the eaves towards the ridge.

Verge and eaves tiles The tiles on a verge are usually nailed and bedded on mortar; eaves tiles are sometimes similarly bedded, but modern practice is simply to nail them. Cracks can usually be filled with mastic, as described for ridge tiles; where damage is more severe, the tiles can be repointed with a mix of one part cement and four parts sand.

4 When replacing a ridge tile, soak it with water and apply mortar along the edges and at the joints. **5** Set tile slips in mortar to close the cavity at the end of a ridge. **6** You will have to lift the first hip tile to gain access to the hip iron. **7** You should be able to replace a single bonnet hip tile by bedding it in mortar. **8** Repair crumbled joints between verge tiles by repointing them with fresh mortar mix

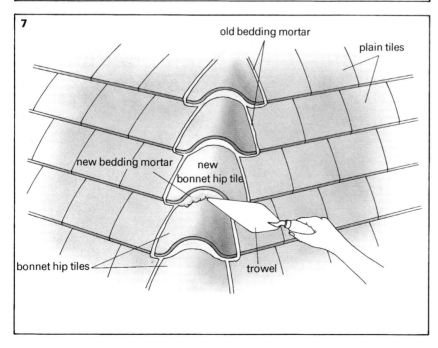

7

old bedding mortar
plain tiles
new bedding mortar
new bonnet hip tile
bonnet hip tiles
trowel

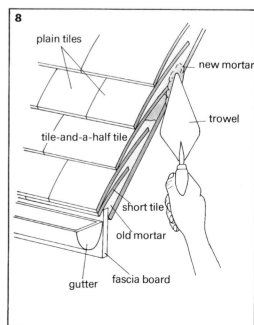

8

plain tiles
new mortar
trowel
tile-and-a-half tile
short tile
old mortar
gutter
fascia board

Repairing a slate roof

A sound roof keeps out water – and thus helps prevent problems caused by damp.
In this section on roof repairs, we describe how to deal with the most common
types of roof damage and look first at slate roofs.

Roof slates deteriorate over a period of time as a result of weathering and movement of the roof structure. If you have slates, check the roof regularly so you can make repairs before the damage lets in water. The first sign of wear may be a hairline crack, or flaking may occur along the edges or round the fixing holes. You should also check for loose slates.

Slates vary in size, shape, thickness and colour, so note your requirements carefully before ordering new slates. It is a good idea to take one of your slates to a builders' merchant to match it up. You can buy second-hand slates from a builders' yard or demolition site, but examine them carefully to make sure they are undamaged. If you cannot get a replacement of the exact size, choose a larger one of the same thickness and cut it to size.

Roof layout Slates are laid from the eaves upwards and each row, known as a course, is overlapped by the one above. The vertical joints of the slates are staggered, so each slate partially covers the two below. The slates are nailed to battens, spaced according to the pitch (or slope) of the roof.

The slates on the first row, at the eaves, and those on the last row, at the ridge, are shorter than those used on the rest of the roof. At the end of every alternate row a wider slate, called a tile-and-a-half, is used to fill the gap left on a straight edge. If the roof is angled at the edge, slates have to be cut to fit. On the edge of a gable roof there may be a narrow slate, known as a verge or creasing slate, which is laid under the slates at the end of each row; these slates give the roof a slight tilt and prevent rainwater running down the wall. V-shaped slates are used for the ridge of the roof.

Drilling and cutting slates
Roof slates may be nailed in the centre or at the top. When replacing slates, use the same nailing position as that of existing slates; to make nail holes, place the old slate over a new one and mark the position of the holes with a nail. Lay the new slate on a piece of wood and make the holes by hammering a nail through or by drilling, using a bit to match the size of the nail to be used.

Above Make regular checks on the condition of your roof. Here not only the slates, but also the roofing battens, have deteriorated badly; both will have to be replaced
1 Layout of a slate roof with details of the ridge (**inset A**), valley (**inset B**), gable end (**inset C**), eaves (**inset D**) and hip (**inset E**)

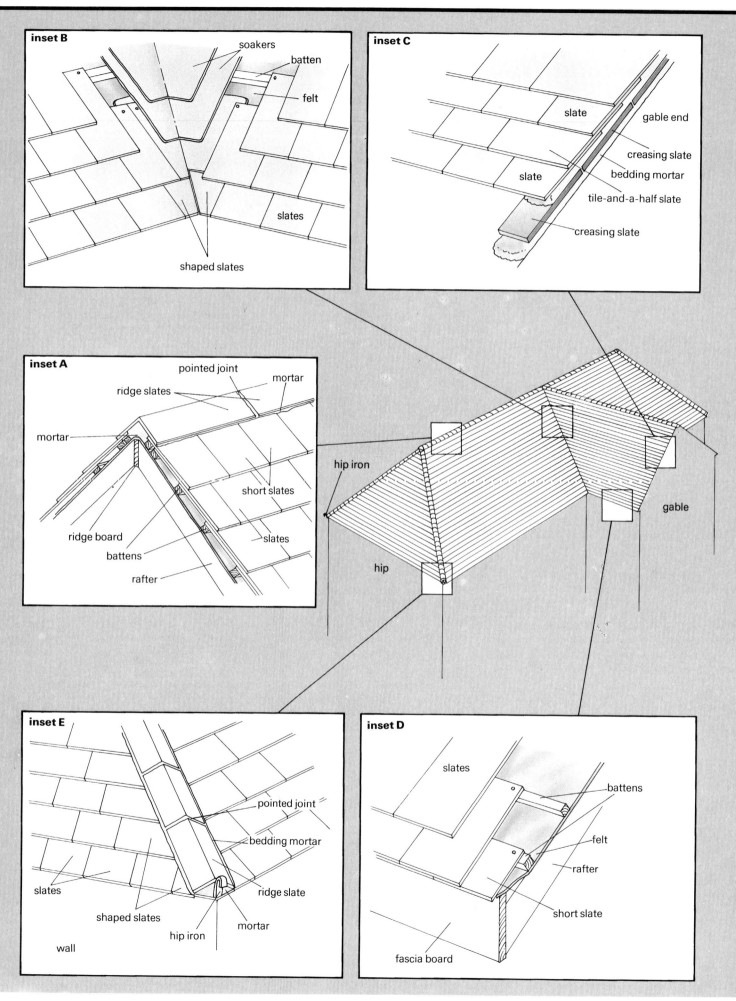

inset B

soakers
batten
felt
slates
shaped slates

inset C

slate
gable end
creasing slate
bedding mortar
tile-and-a-half slate
slate
creasing slate

inset A

pointed joint
mortar
ridge slates
mortar
short slates
ridge board
slates
battens
rafter

hip iron
hip
gable

inset E

pointed joint
bedding mortar
ridge slate
slates
shaped slates
hip iron
mortar
wall

inset D

slates
battens
felt
rafter
short slate
slates
fascia board

If you need to cut a slate, score the cutting line on both sides with the point of a trowel. If you are cutting a large slate down to a smaller size, use an old slate as a guide. To mark out a shape – for example, to fit the angled edge of a roof – use the old slate as a guide (if it is not too badly damaged) or make a template. Place the marked slate on a firm, flat surface with the waste section overhanging. Chop halfway along the cutting line with the sharp edge of a trowel, then turn the slate over and work in from the other end so the cuts meet in the middle. Never try to snap the slate along the cutting line.

Replacing a damaged slate

When removing a single slate, take care not to damage surrounding slates. If the fixing nails have corroded through, you will be able to pull the slate away quite easily. To remove a securely nailed slate, use a slate ripper. Slide the claw of the ripper under the damaged slate and hook it round the nails. Pull the ripper to break the nails and carefully take out the old slate, making sure you do not dislodge adjacent slates.

You cannot nail down a single replacement slate, since the fixing holes will be overlapped by the slates above. To fix it you need a strip of lead about 250mm (10in) wide; nail one end of the strip to the batten between the nails of the two exposed slates. You will need to lift the edge of the slate above; be careful not to crack it. Slide the new slate into position under the overlapping ones, lining up the edge with adjacent slates, and bend up the free end of the lead strip to hold the slate in place.

Ridge slates These are bedded down in mortar. Remove any loose ridge slates for refitting and take away any damaged ones. If you need access to the top batten for fixing the top row of replacement slates, remove the relevant ridge slates. To remove securely fixed ridge slates, loosen the mortar under the slates with a sharp brick bolster. Hold the bolster parallel to the slate and tap it with a club hammer. Clean away old mortar from the top course of slates in the same way and chip away mortar from any ridge slates which are to be relaid.

For relaying ridge slates, mix a mortar of one part cement to three or four parts sand. Lay the fresh mortar along the ridge with a trowel and roughen the surface. Place the ridge slates on the mortar and tap them level with adjacent slates. Fill the joints between the slates with mortar and also press mortar along the bottom of the slates; then smooth off with a trowel. If you have to fit a whole new ridge, you may find it cheaper to use clay ridge tiles rather than slate ones.

Repairing large areas

Rotten battens may cause damage to a large area of slates. If you have to carry out major repairs, erect scaffolding and secure crawling boards to the working area to ensure safety and avoid damage.

2a Use a hammer and a nail to make fixing holes in a new slate
2b Alternatively use an electric drill
3a When cutting a large slate to size, use an old slate as a guide
3b To shape slates, make a card or hardboard template; again use an old slate (**inset**) as a guide

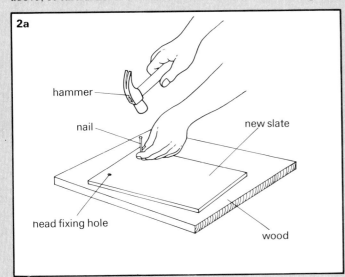

2a

hammer

nail

new slate

head fixing hole

wood

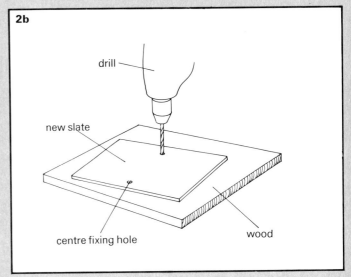

2b

drill

new slate

centre fixing hole

wood

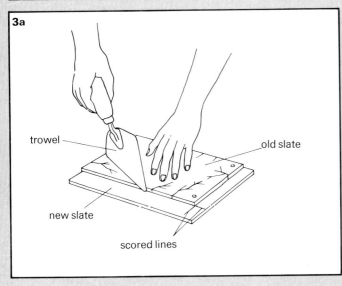

3a

trowel

old slate

new slate

scored lines

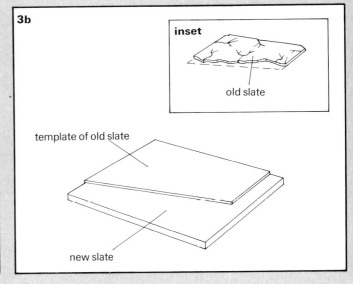

3b

inset

old slate

template of old slate

new slate

4a

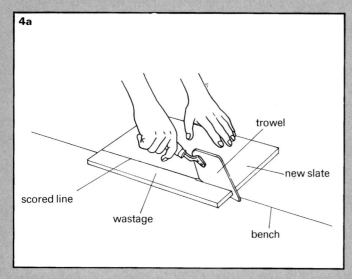

scored line

wastage

trowel

new slate

bench

4b

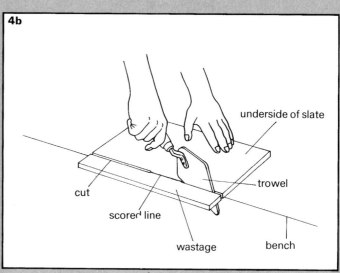

underside of slate

cut

scored line

wastage

trowel

bench

5

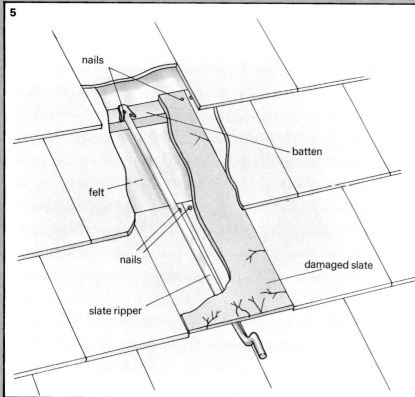

nails

batten

felt

nails

slate ripper

damaged slate

6a

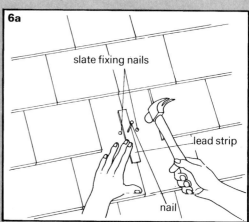

slate fixing nails

lead strip

nail

6b

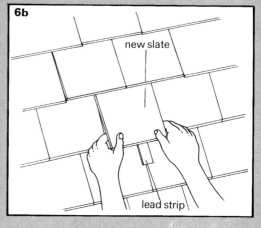

new slate

lead strip

6c

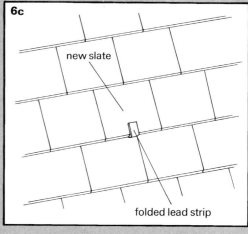

new slate

folded lead strip

4a Cut slates with a trowel; work from one end to the centre; 4b Turn the slate over and work from the other end to finish the cut. 5 Remove slates with a slate ripper. 6a To replace a single slate, first fix a lead strip to the batten between the nails of the two exposed slates; 6b Lift the slates immediately above and slide the new slate into position; 6c Bend the end of the lead strip over the slate to hold it in place. 7 Loosen the bedding mortar of ridge slates with a bolster. 8 Saw through rotten battens where they cross the rafters

Remove all the slates from the damaged area and stack the undamaged ones carefully. Remove any unsound battens by sawing through them diagonally where they cross the rafters.

Cut new lengths of the same size softwood as the existing battens – usually 50×25mm (2×1in) – at a matching angle to provide a tight fit; fix the new battens with a 50mm (2in) nail at each end. If there is any bituminous felt which is damaged, repair it before you fit the battens in place. Cut the torn piece to a neat rectangle, fit a larger rectangle of new felt over it and stick it down with bitumen adhesive. Coat all new timber and the surrounding old structure with a wood preservative before replacing the slates.

Fixing slates Start at the eaves with a row of short slates. If you are making the repair in the middle of an existing row, slide the first new slate under the last overlapping slate, placing the holes over the centre of the batten. Secure the exposed part

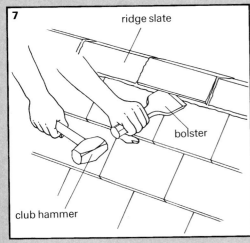

7

ridge slate

bolster

club hammer

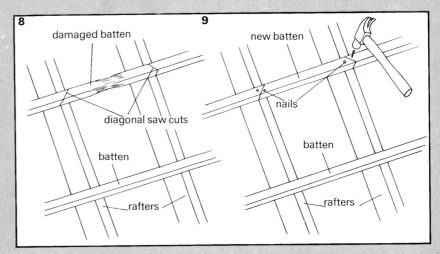

8

9

damaged batten

diagonal saw cuts

batten

rafters

new batten

nails

batten

rafters

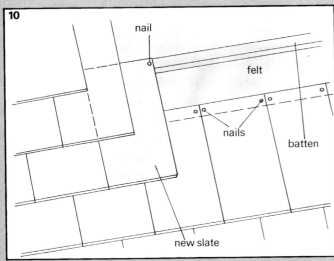

10

nail

felt

nails

batten

new slate

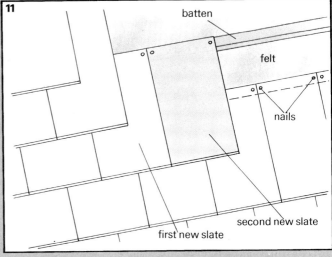

11

batten

felt

nails

second new slate

first new slate

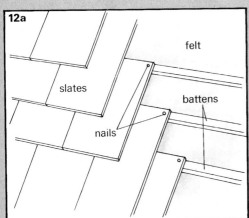

12a

felt

slates

battens

nails

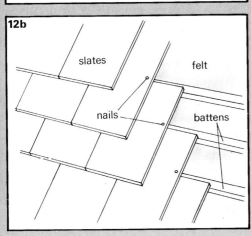

12b

slates

felt

nails

battens

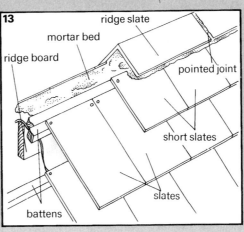

13

ridge slate

mortar bed

ridge board

pointed joint

short slates

slates

battens

of the slate with a nail driven into the batten. Butt-join the remaining slates in the row and fix each one with two nails, lining up the upper edges.

The second row will completely cover the row of short slates (this gives extra protection against damp). Fix the slates as for the first row, covering the vertical joins of the slates below. Continue fixing the slates, moving up the roof one course at a time. All vertical joins should be covered and each course should overlap the one below.

Unless you are reslating to the ridge of the roof, the nail holes of the last few slates will be covered by the overlapping slates above, so use lead strips to fix these in position, as described earlier. If you are working right up to the ridge, you will have to remove the ridge slates to fix the top row of slates.

9 Fix replacement battens with a nail at each end
10 To replace slates in the middle of an existing row, slide the first new slate under the last overlapping one; place the holes over the centre of the batten and secure with a nail
11 Butt-join the second slate and secure it with two nails; fix the remaining slates in the course in the same way
12a When replacing head-nailed slates, line up the top of the slates with the top of the battens
12b For centre-nailed slates, position the top edge of the slates in the centre of the batten above
13 Ridge slates will have to be removed when replacing the top row

Repairing flashings and valleys

If flashings (weatherproofing where the roof joins walls, chimney stacks or roof windows) or valley linings (weatherproofing at the junction of two sloping roof surfaces) become defective, the first signs of trouble may be spoiled ceiling decoration or damp patches on chimney-breast walls due to rainwater penetration. Check these areas of the roof regularly, making any repairs as soon as possible, and you should be able to stop the trouble before it gets too bad. Many repairs are simple and ones you can do yourself.

Flashings

Traditionally flashings are made from sheets of lead or zinc; but other corrosion-resistant materials, such as aluminium alloy, copper, bituminous felt and rigid bitumen-asbestos, are also used. A fairly recent development is the self-adhesive flashing strip; this is available in various widths and is cheaper and easier to fit than most traditional materials. These flashing strips usually consist of heavy duty reflective aluminium foil, coated on one side with a thick layer of specially formulated pressure-sensitive bitumen adhesive. The adhesive surface is protected with a siliconized release paper which you peel off just before applying the flashing. In some cases the aluminium foil is coated with a grey vinyl lacquer, so it looks like lead.

Making repairs

If flashings are torn or cracked, clean the damaged area thoroughly with a wire brush and go over it with emery paper. You can then cover the crack or tear with a patch of self-adhesive flashing strip: simply peel off the paper backing and smooth the strip firmly into place. Alternatively press thick bitumen mastic into each crack so there is about 1.5mm ($\frac{1}{16}$in) of mastic over the crack and over-lapping it by about 1.5mm ($\frac{1}{16}$in) all round. Lay a piece of aluminium foil or thin roofing felt over each repair and press the edges into the mastic. Apply another layer of mastic and brush liquid bitumen proofing over the entire flashings.

Repointing Along its top edge, metal flashing is tucked into the mortar joints of the brickwork; if the joints are defective and the flashing comes away from them, rainwater will trickle behind and eventually seep through the roof. To repoint the joints, first rake out the old mortar with a cold chisel and club hammer, then tuck the flashing back in place, wedging it at intervals with scraps of lead or small pieces of timber. Dampen the joint with water and fill it with a mix of four parts sand to one part cement.

Replacing flashings

Flashings which are badly corroded are best replaced with new material; the method of replacement varies with the type of flashing and the material used.

Stepped flashing With a single lap tiled roof (and some slate roofs) the flashing at the side of the chimney is usually stepped and dressed (pressed down) over the tiles. Stepped flashing is inserted in the mortar joints all the way down the side of the chimney and it is difficult to replace in the same way. However, you can apply a self-adhesive flashing

1a Rainwater will seep through your roof if flashings are damaged; having cleaned the area, press mastic into the damaged area and push on a piece of foil or roofing felt
1b Apply another layer of mastic over the patch and brush liquid bitumen over the whole flashing
2 If flashings come away from the brickwork, rake out the old mortar and wedge the flashing back into the wall with timber pegs; refill with fresh mortar

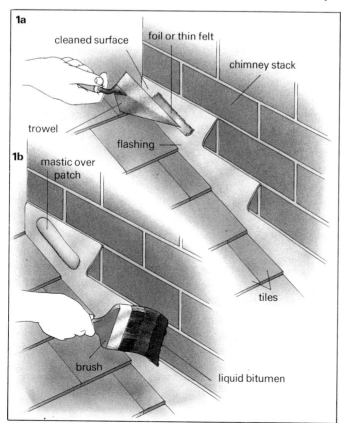

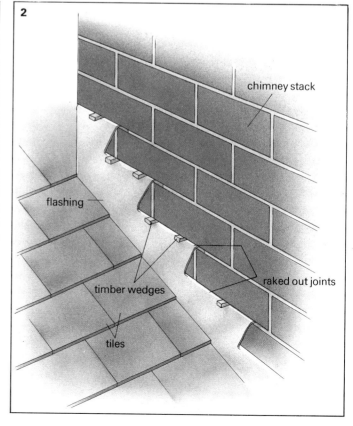

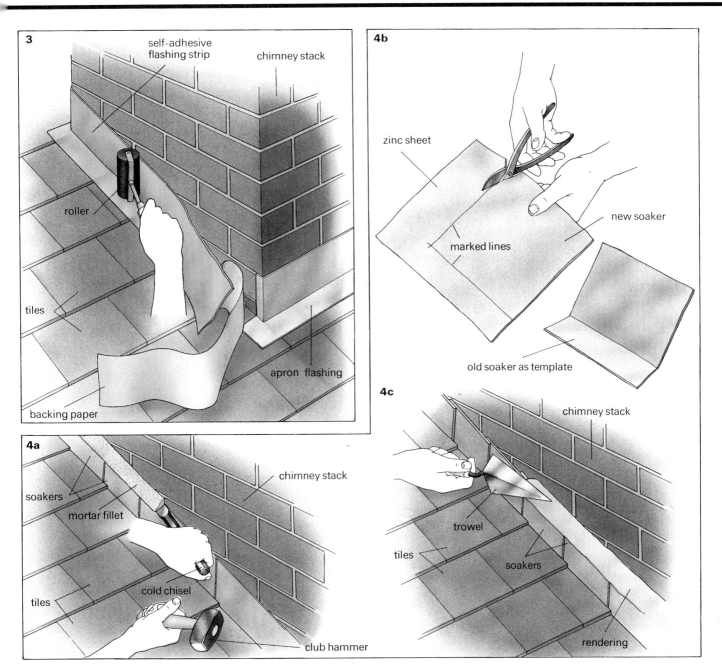

3 self-adhesive flashing strip

chimney stack

roller

tiles

backing paper

apron flashing

4b

zinc sheet

marked lines

new soaker

old soaker as template

4c

chimney stack

trowel

tiles

soakers

rendering

4a

soakers

mortar fillet

chimney stack

tiles

cold chisel

club hammer

strip which does not need stepping or inserting in the mortar joints. Carefully lever out the old flashing and thoroughly clean the area with a wire brush; you can then apply a primer as recommended by the manufacturer – this is not essential, but it does ensure the strip adheres firmly to the brickwork. Cut the strip to length with a pair of scissors and carefully peel off the backing paper; press the strip into place and smooth it down with a cloth pad or a wood seam roller as used for wallpapering, making sure there are no gaps between the strip and the surface.

Soakers On a double lap (or plain) tiled roof – and again on some slate roofs – the flashing at the side of the chimney and against parapet walls usually consists of separate pieces of metal, called soakers, interleaved with the tiles. The soakers are turned up against the wall or side of the chimney and a stepped flashing or mortar fillet covers their up-turned edges. To replace faulty soakers, chip away the old mortar fillet, or lever out the flashing, and rake out the joints between the bricks to about 19mm ($\frac{3}{4}$in). Remove adjacent tiles, numbering

them as you work to enable you to replace them in the correct order, and remove the damaged soakers – again numbering them as you do so. Cut pieces of zinc to the shape of the soakers, using the old ones as templates. If you intend to use self-adhesive flashing dampen the raked out joints with water, repoint, and replace the soakers, interleaving them with the tiles in the same way as they were originally fitted. You can now apply the flashing over the soakers, as described above. If you intend to apply rendering over the soakers and to the wall above, leave the mortar joints open to provide a key for the rendering. Use a mix of four parts sand to one part cement and trowel on the mortar to a thickness of 13mm ($\frac{1}{2}$in). Score the surface to ensure good adhesion, leave the render to dry and apply a second coat, again 13mm ($\frac{1}{2}$in) thick.

Straight flashings When replacing straight, horizontal flashings of traditional materials, such as lead or zinc, lever out the damaged flashing and rake out the mortar joints to about 25mm (1in). Cut the lead or zinc sheet to the required length, lay it over a batten and bend over a 20mm (or $\frac{3}{4}$in) strip

3 Replace stepped flashing with self-adhesive strip; peel off the backing paper and roll down the strip
4a When replacing faulty soakers, chip off mortar fillet
4b Cut the new soakers, with old ones as templates
4c Apply render over the soakers and the mortar joints
5a When replacing straight flashing, bend the edge of the new strip over a batten
5b Use a sliding bevel to check the required angle
5c Shape the metal to the correct angle
5d Fit the new flashing strip into the dampened mortar joint, hammering the lower half to match the roof slope
6 Seal cracks in cement fillet with non-hardening mastic

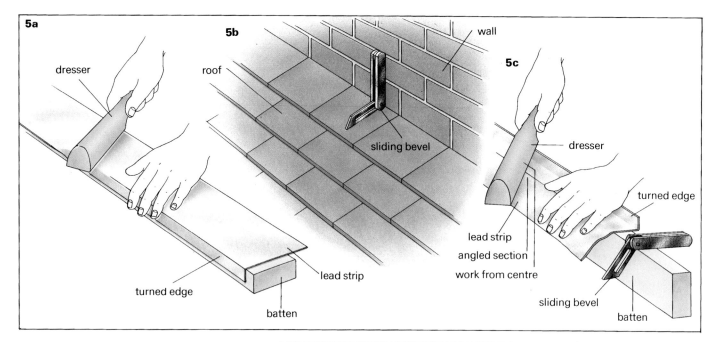

5a dresser
5b roof wall
sliding bevel
turned edge
lead strip
batten

5c dresser
turned edge
lead strip
angled section
work from centre
sliding bevel
batten

at right-angles down one long edge. Use a sliding bevel to determine the angle between the roof and the wall; turn the sheet over and shape it to match the angle on the bevel, working from the centre of the sheet outwards. Dampen the mortar joints with water and insert the angled section of the new flashing in the joint, packing with small wedges of zinc or lead at both ends and overlapping joins in the flashing by about 150mm (6in). Gently hammer the lower half of the flashing to match the slope of the roof then fill the joint with fresh mortar. Finally remove surplus mortar with the point of a trowel.

Alternatively you can replace this type of flashing with a self-adhesive strip, as described for stepped flashing.

Cement fillets Occasionally the flashing round the base of a chimney or against a parapet wall is made from a triangular fillet of cement mortar; it is quite common for this type of flashing to crack where it joins the wall. If the damage is not severe, seal the gap with a non-hardening mastic; if the fillet is in bad condition, it is best to chip the fillet away and replace it with a self-adhesive flashing strip.

Valley linings

Lead, zinc and aluminium are all commonly used for valley linings. Small cracks and holes can be repaired in the same way as for metal flashings; but after making such repairs, it is important to seal the entire valley with liquid bitumen proofing or liquid plastic coating.

Replacing valley linings .
If the valley lining is severely corroded or wrinkled, it must be replaced; this involves lifting several tiles at each side of the valley, so have a tarpaulin or heavy duty polythene sheeting ready to cover the roof in case of rain. You can replace the lining with zinc or lead sheet or use roofing felt; but the simplest method is to apply a wide self-adhesive flashing strip.

Zinc or lead lining Remove the tiles covering the valley edge at each side, numbering them so you can replace them in the correct order. Lever up the old lining and lower it carefully to the ground, then remove the fixing nails with pincers. Check the

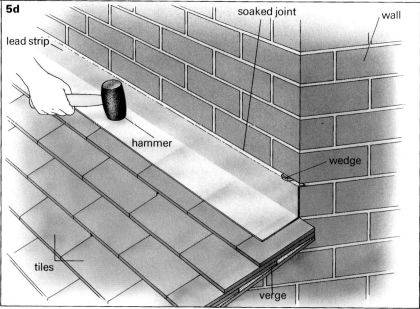

5d lead strip
soaked joint
wall
hammer
wedge
tiles
verge

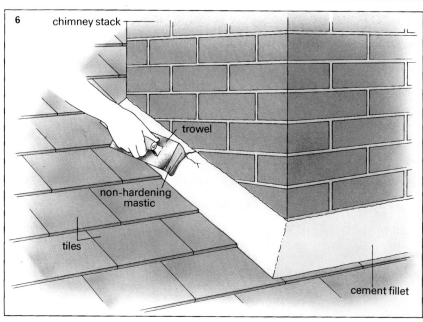

6 chimney stack
trowel
non-hardening mastic
tiles
cement fillet

timber underlining is securely fixed and coat it with creosote for protection. Cut the replacement zinc or lead to length, allowing for a 50mm (2in) overlap at the eaves, and place it over the underlining; press the lining down firmly to fit the angle of the valley and hold it in place with galvanized nails. If you have to use more than one sheet of metal, make sure the sheets overlap by about 225mm (9in). Where the lining meets the junction of the roof and wall, shape the end to match the junction, allowing a 75mm (3in) turning against the wall. Fix the sheet to the battens at both sides using galvanized nails, then relay the tiles; work from the eaves upwards and make sure you replace the tiles in the correct order. Finally apply self-adhesive flashing strip at the junction of the roof and wall to guard against rainwater penetration.

Felt lining You can replace an old metal lining with three layers of roofing felt. Remove the tiles and old lining as before and cut the felt to length. Fix the first layer of felt to the valley underlining, using galvanized nails, and fix the second and third layers with felt adhesive. Then replace the tiles in their original positions.

Valley tiles The major concrete roof tile manufacturers now produce special valley tiles which can be used as a cheaper alternative to the traditional lining materials. However, the method of fixing these tiles involves modifying the tile battening on each side of the valley, and the financial saving on materials may therefore be more than offset by the loss of time involved in carrying out the necessary modifications to the structure before the tiles can be positioned.

7a When replacing valley linings, remove the tiles on each side and fit felt onto the battens
7b Cover the felt with lead sheet nailed to alternate battens
7c Shape the lead sheet to fit the corner of the walls
7d Replace tiles from the eaves upwards
7e Apply self-adhesive flashing at the wall joins
8 Three layers of felt can be used instead of lead; nail the first layer and glue the other two

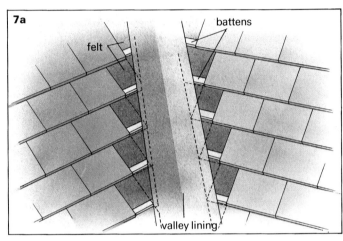

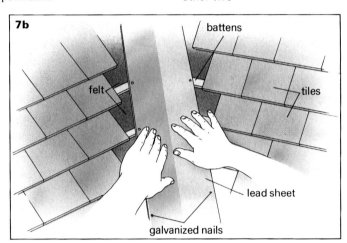

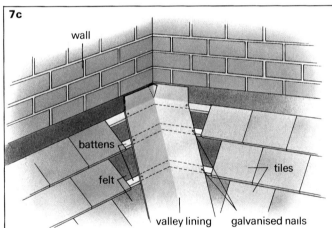

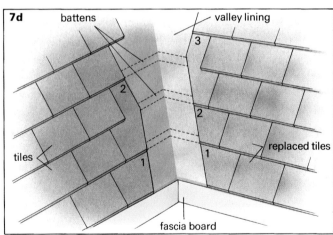

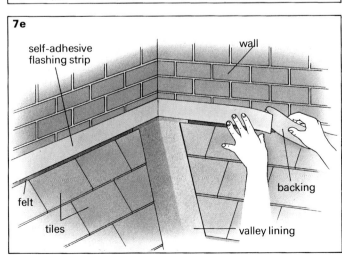

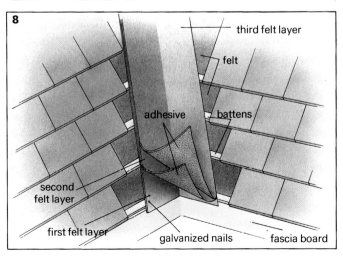

Repairing roof boards and snowguards

Where you are repairing a roof covering you should check the structure around it is in sound condition; damage in this area will shorten the life of the covering. Sometimes it may be sufficient to patch the damaged areas. Barge boards, fascias and soffits, for example, which have only slightly rotted can be temporarily repaired by scraping away the rotten timber, filling the cavity with an exterior grade filler and painting thoroughly with a waterproof paint. In slightly more serious cases the affected section should be cut out and replaced with a new piece of timber. For a lasting repair and where the damage is too bad for patching, the boards should be replaced.

Replacing boards

Before you begin, remember these boards are heavier than they look from the ground and you should attempt replacement only if you can work from a scaffold.

Fascias and soffits Fascia boards, to which the gutters are fixed, cover the ends of rafters and a soffit board seals the gap underneath, between the wall and the fascia. To replace fascias and soffits, take off the gutters and gutter brackets and remove

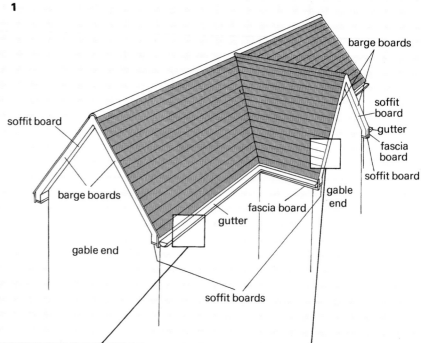

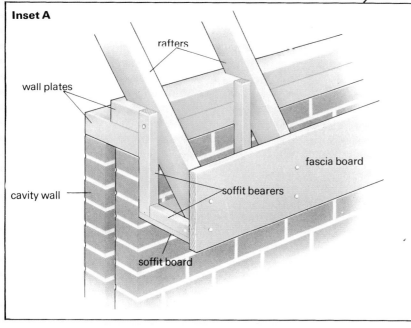

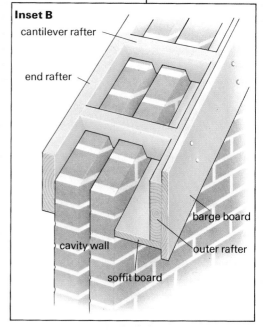

the fascia by prising it away from the rafter ends with a cold chisel or wrecking bar. The soffit is nailed to the rafter ends and supported by a batten plugged and screwed to the wall or by bearers nailed to the rafters. If the soffit supports are sound, simply prise away the soffit; where the soffit is fixed to bearers you will have to remove the fixing nails partially to release the soffit. If the soffit supports are rotten, these too should be removed and replaced; where the fixings which hold these in place are too difficult to remove, you can cut out the rotten sections with a panel saw and replace them with pieces of new timber.

Where rafter ends are rotten you may be able to form new ends by bolting pieces of new timber alongside the decayed rafters. If this is impossible,

the ends should be removed and replaced.

Treat all the roof timbers with wood preservative before fixing the new boards. Cut the soffits and fascias to length; if you have to join several lengths to make up a long run, check the joints coincide with the centre lines of the rafters and make the saw cuts at an angle of 45 degrees to ensure neat joints. Hold the soffit in position; if there is a definite gap between the wall and the soffit, you will have to cut the soffit to the shape of the wall so make sure the board is wide enough. To mark the cutting line on the soffit, hold a pencil against a scrap of wood and move this along the wall, tracing the contour of the wall onto the soffit. Trim the edge of the soffit to match, making an allowance for the width of the block of wood.

1 Locating the position of soffit boards, fascias and barge boards
Inset A Detail of the fascia fixing at the eaves
Inset B Detail of the barge board fixing at the verge

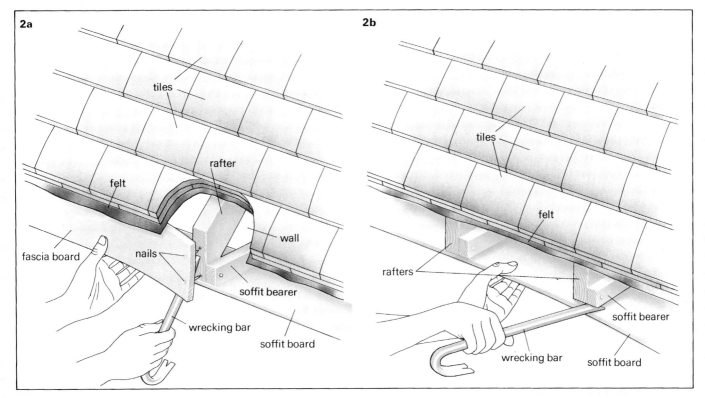

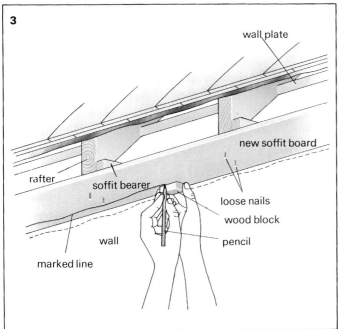

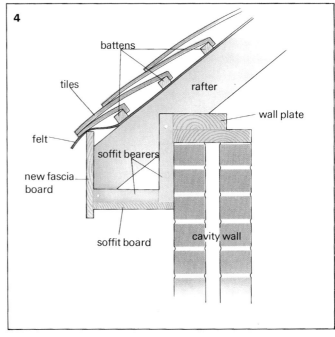

2a Removing the fascia
2b Levering the soffit
away from its bearers
3 Tracing the wall outline
onto the new soffit
4 Fitting the new soffit
and fascia

Treat the new boards with wood preservative and apply a wood primer. Replace the soffit by fixing it to the underside of the rafter ends and supports with galvanized nails. Fix the new fascia by nailing it to the rafter ends and through the edge of the soffit. The top edge of the fascia should tuck under the overhang of the roof slates or tiles and any underfelt should overhang the front of the fascia so it can be tucked into the gutters later. The lower edge of the fascia should protrude below the face of the soffit to protect the soffit and the walls.

Barge boards These are fitted at the gable end of the roof. They are screwed to the roof timbers and, like the fascia board, incorporate a soffit which seals the gap underneath. Lever out the old boards with a crowbar or wrecking bar, starting at the

eaves and working upwards. Use the old boards as a guide to cut the new ones to the correct angle at the ridge; alternatively make a card template of the angle before removing the boards and transfer the shape to the new boards, trimming as necessary. Treat the boards with clear wood preservative and allow this to dry, then prime all surfaces. Fix the soffit to the underside of the roof timbers, using rustproof screws, then fit the barge board over the soffit and screw it to the roof timbers. After fixing, you may find you have to seal the verge by re-pointing the tiles.

Repairing snowguards
Usually these consist of a strip of galvanized steel mesh fixed to support brackets which are screwed

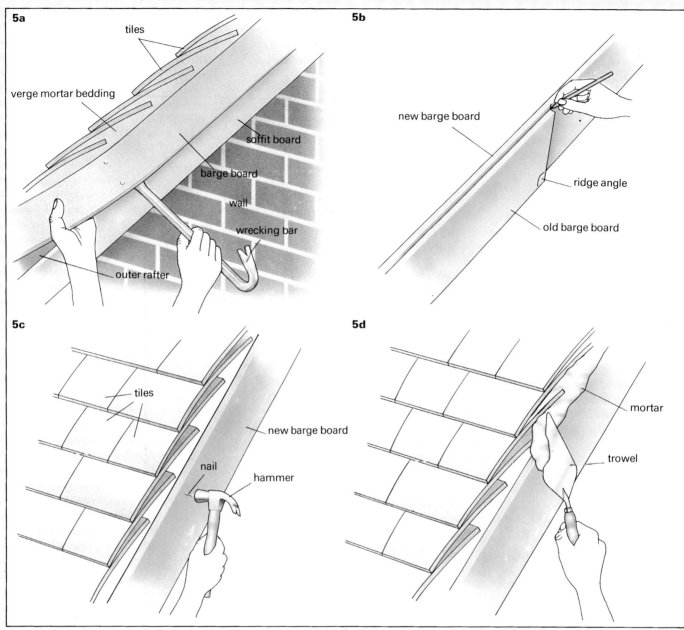

5a
- tiles
- verge mortar bedding
- soffit board
- barge board
- wall
- wrecking bar
- outer rafter

5b
- new barge board
- ridge angle
- old barge board

5c
- tiles
- new barge board
- nail
- hammer

5d
- tiles
- mortar
- trowel
- new barge board

to the sides of the rafters or to the fascia board. Where the mesh has come loose, refix it to the supports with twists of copper or galvanized steel wire. If the mesh has corroded, remove the fixings which hold it in place and, after lifting away the mesh, replace it with galvanized steel mesh fixed to the roof side of the support brackets with wire twists. Remove any loose brackets and refix them in a slightly different position so the fixing screws can bite into new wood. If brackets are bent, you can straighten them by using a length of strong tube as a lever, slipping it over the bracket.

Warning For safety reasons, you should always work from a secure foothold, such as a scaffold tower cantilevered over the roof or a ladder which is securely tied at the top.

5a Removing an old barge board with a wrecking bar
5b Using the old board as a guide to mark the shape of the new board
5c Nailing the new board in place
5d Repointing the tiles at the verge
6 Repositioning loose snowguard brackets

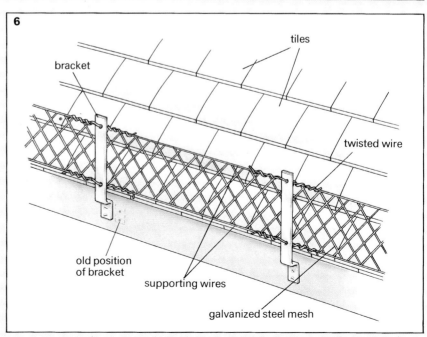

6
- bracket
- tiles
- twisted wire
- old position of bracket
- supporting wires
- galvanized steel mesh

Repairing gutters

Plastic or cast iron guttering comes in three shapes
1 Half-round, to rest in brackets fixed to fascia board, rafters or brickwork
2 Square, fixed as above
3 Ogee, to be screwed direct to fascia, or rest on brackets as shown here

1

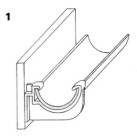

2

3

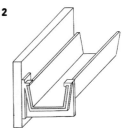

Defective rainwater systems cause all sorts of damp problems in the house structure. Water constantly pouring down an outside wall will eventually penetrate inside, ruining the decoration and causing mould growth. So it is important to keep your guttering in good repair. If you are prompted now to check your guttering for the first time, you may have a fair amount of work on hand to get it into shape. But once the repair work has been done, maintenance is a simple yearly task.

If you need an extra incentive to start immediately, remember if you allow things to deteriorate you may have to call in a professional to repair the guttering or even to replace the complete system and this would prove expensive. The best time to check the gutters is in the late autumn, once all the leaves have fallen. If you have already noticed leaks or damp patches, make the job a priority.

Working at height is not to everyone's liking. Use a secure ladder or make the job easier with a scaffolding system (available from hire shops). When working on metal gutters, wear an old pair of gloves to guard against cuts from sharp edges.

Types of gutter

In the past cast iron was the most common material for guttering, but plastic is now widely used. Today you cannot easily obtain a complete cast iron system, although you can buy replacement parts. Cast iron guttering comes in three shapes: half-round, square and ogee (a cross between half-round and square section). Half-round and square types rest in brackets fixed to the fascia board, rafters or brickwork. Ogee section can either be screwed direct to the fascia or be supported on brackets. The joints are sealed together with red lead, putty or other suitable jointing mastic and secured with bolts.

Plastic rainwater systems have a distinct advantage over cast iron ones since plastic is light, durable and needs little or no decoration. Plastic guttering is made in half-round, ogee and square sections which fit into special brackets. The lengths are joined together with clips housing rubber seals, or gaskets, to make them waterproof; a jointing cement is sometimes used instead of, or in addition to, the gasket.

Gutter blockages

Scoop out the rubbish with a trowel or a piece of card shaped to the profile of the gutter. Don't use the downpipe as a rubbish chute as it may become blocked or the rubbish sink into the drain.

Flush out the gutter with water; it should flow steadily towards the downpipe. If it overflows at the entrance then the downpipe is blocked and needs to be cleared.

If the downpipe gets blocked tie a small bundle of rags to the end of a pole and use this as a plunger to push away any obstruction. Place a bowl at the outlet on the ground to prevent rubbish sinking into the drain. If there is a 'swan neck' between the gutter and the downpipe, use a length of stiff wire to clear it of debris. To prevent further blockages, fit a cage into the entrance of the downpipe. You

---

Basic items
drill, hammer and screwdriver

For clearing blockages
trowel or piece of card
pole or stiff wire, rags and bowl
wire or plastic netting (to prevent blockages)

For realigning
string line, spirit level (if used)
nails 150mm (6in) long
No 8 chrome-plated round head screws 37mm (1½in) long
wall plugs

For treating rust
wire brush or electric drill with wire cup brush
rust killer, rust-resistant primer

epoxy repair material
fine glasspaper

For repairing joints
epoxy repair material
medium glasspaper
mastic sealer or replacement gasket

For replacing a section
nails (to locate bolt holes)
rust killer
penetrating oil or hacksaw (to remove bolts)
old chisel (to scrape off)
metal putty
rust-resistant primer
aluminium primer (over bituminous coatings)
undercoat and top coat paint

equipment

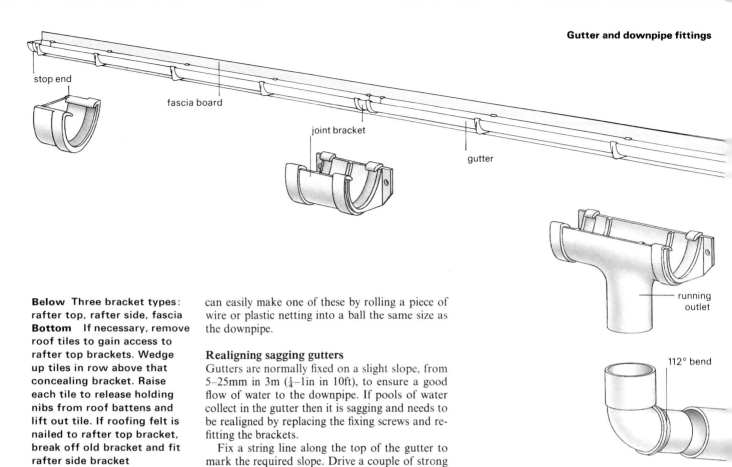

stop end

fascia board

joint bracket

gutter

running outlet

112° bend

Below Three bracket types: rafter top, rafter side, fascia **Bottom** If necessary, remove roof tiles to gain access to rafter top brackets. Wedge up tiles in row above that concealing bracket. Raise each tile to release holding nibs from roof battens and lift out tile. If roofing felt is nailed to rafter top bracket, break off old bracket and fit rafter side bracket

can easily make one of these by rolling a piece of wire or plastic netting into a ball the same size as the downpipe.

Realigning sagging gutters
Gutters are normally fixed on a slight slope, from 5–25mm in 3m ($\frac{1}{4}$–1in in 10ft), to ensure a good flow of water to the downpipe. If pools of water collect in the gutter then it is sagging and needs to be realigned by replacing the fixing screws and re-fitting the brackets.

Fix a string line along the top of the gutter to mark the required slope. Drive a couple of strong nails into the fascia about 25mm (1in) below the gutter for support while it is being refitted. Take out the old fixing screws (if these are in the edges of the rafters you may have to remove a tile from the roof to gain access to them). Now release the brackets so the gutter rests on the support nails; tap wall plugs into the old screw holes and refix the brackets using new screws. Pack the gutter up to the required height with bits of timber placed between it and the support nails. Finally remove nails and string line.

Rust and cracks
Inspect metal systems for any signs of rust and clean back with a wire brush or, if you have an extension lead, with an electric drill fitted with a wire cup brush – this saves a lot of hard work. Now treat the cleaned areas with a rust killer.

Fill hairline cracks with two coats of rust-resistant primer. Fill definite cracks or holes with an epoxy (water-resistant) repair material. Rub down with fine glasspaper.

Corrosion is always worst at the back edge of the gutter and to repair this you will have to dismantle the system and treat each section separately.

Leaking joints
Seal leaking joints in metal gutters with an epoxy repair material and rub down. If a leak develops at the joints of a plastic system, release the affected section by squeezing it at one end and lifting it clear of the adjoining length. If the gasket in the joint is sound, simply replace the section making sure the spigot end butts tightly against the socket of the adjoining piece. If the gasket is worn, scrape away all the old material and insert a replacement gasket or apply three good strips of mastic sealer in its place. Then press the two sections together again.

Support brackets

rafter top bracket

rafter side bracket

fascia bracket

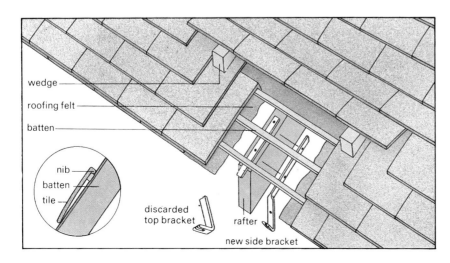

wedge

roofing felt

batten

nib

batten

tile

discarded top bracket

rafter

new side bracket

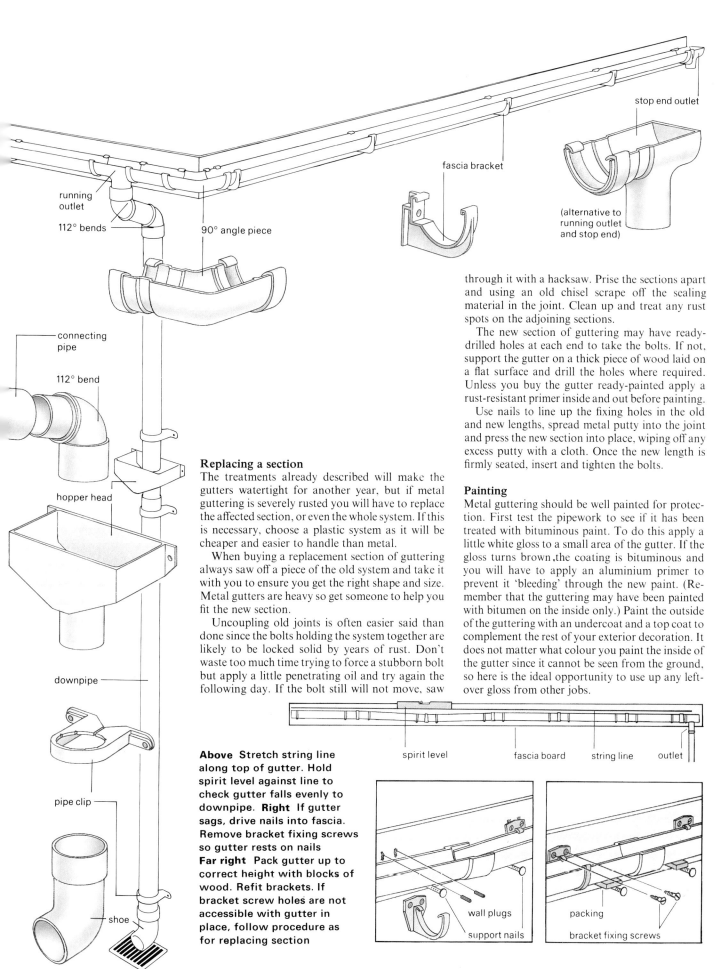

stop end outlet

fascia bracket

(alternative to
running outlet
and stop end)

running
outlet

112° bends

90° angle piece

connecting
pipe

112° bend

hopper head

downpipe

pipe clip

shoe

through it with a hacksaw. Prise the sections apart
and using an old chisel scrape off the sealing
material in the joint. Clean up and treat any rust
spots on the adjoining sections.

The new section of guttering may have ready-
drilled holes at each end to take the bolts. If not,
support the gutter on a thick piece of wood laid on
a flat surface and drill the holes where required.
Unless you buy the gutter ready-painted apply a
rust-resistant primer inside and out before painting.

Use nails to line up the fixing holes in the old
and new lengths, spread metal putty into the joint
and press the new section into place, wiping off any
excess putty with a cloth. Once the new length is
firmly seated, insert and tighten the bolts.

Replacing a section

The treatments already described will make the
gutters watertight for another year, but if metal
guttering is severely rusted you will have to replace
the affected section, or even the whole system. If this
is necessary, choose a plastic system as it will be
cheaper and easier to handle than metal.

When buying a replacement section of guttering
always saw off a piece of the old system and take it
with you to ensure you get the right shape and size.
Metal gutters are heavy so get someone to help you
fit the new section.

Uncoupling old joints is often easier said than
done since the bolts holding the system together are
likely to be locked solid by years of rust. Don't
waste too much time trying to force a stubborn bolt
but apply a little penetrating oil and try again the
following day. If the bolt still will not move, saw

Painting

Metal guttering should be well painted for protection. First test the pipework to see if it has been
treated with bituminous paint. To do this apply a
little white gloss to a small area of the gutter. If the
gloss turns brown,the coating is bituminous and
you will have to apply an aluminium primer to
prevent it 'bleeding' through the new paint. (Remember that the guttering may have been painted
with bitumen on the inside only.) Paint the outside
of the guttering with an undercoat and a top coat to
complement the rest of your exterior decoration. It
does not matter what colour you paint the inside of
the gutter since it cannot be seen from the ground,
so here is the ideal opportunity to use up any left-
over gloss from other jobs.

spirit level   fascia board   string line   outlet

Above Stretch string line
along top of gutter. Hold
spirit level against line to
check gutter falls evenly to
downpipe. **Right** If gutter
sags, drive nails into fascia.
Remove bracket fixing screws
so gutter rests on nails
Far right Pack gutter up to
correct height with blocks of
wood. Refit brackets. If
bracket screw holes are not
accessible with gutter in
place, follow procedure as
for replacing section

wall plugs

support nails

packing

bracket fixing screws

Repairing flat, shed and corrugated roofs

While the most common type of house roof is pitched and covered with tiles or slates, there are other kinds of covering and you may have one on your property. The main roof can be flat rather than pitched or there may be a flat roof on a room extension, garage or other small-scale construction: some roofs are corrugated and you may have a shed with a roof covered in roofing felt. Whatever the type of roof, it is worth checking for signs of deterioration – where repairs are needed, it may be possible for you to carry them out yourself.

Flat roofs
A faulty roof may be indicated by a damp patch on a ceiling. Tracing the source of a leak in a flat roof can be difficult since water may have travelled some distance before it shows as a damp patch. Therefore looking at a roof directly above a damp patch will not necessarily show where the problem lies and you should examine the entire roof for damage.

If the roof looks in reasonable condition, it should be sufficient to apply two coats of heavy duty liquid bitumen coating to waterproof it. Alternatively you can apply an overall plastic membrane to the roof surface. Both treatments can be carried out on roofing felt, asphalt, zinc, lead or concrete.

Bitumen proofing Before applying this water-proofing liquid, remove dirt and dust with a wire brush and a knife or wallpaper scraper and sweep the roof to remove debris. If there is any moss and lichen, scrape it off and treat the roof surface with a proprietary fungicide solution, allowing this to dry before carrying out the waterproofing treatment. Bitumen proofing can be applied by brush to damp as well as dry surfaces; you will find dipping the brush in water from time to time makes it easier to spread the bitumen. Make sure the first coat is thoroughly dry before applying the second.

Where there is more serious damage to the roof

1a Before laying new felt, remove the old felt by cutting round the edges and tearing it off; trim round fixing nails as necessary
1b Nail battens to the top of the fascia boards to form drip rails. If the fascia board projects upwards at the verge, also nail an angled timber fillet to the inside of the board
1c Use nails to fix the first layer of felt, working from the centre outwards
1d Fix the second layer of felt using adhesive; make sure the joints do not coincide with the joints of the first layer

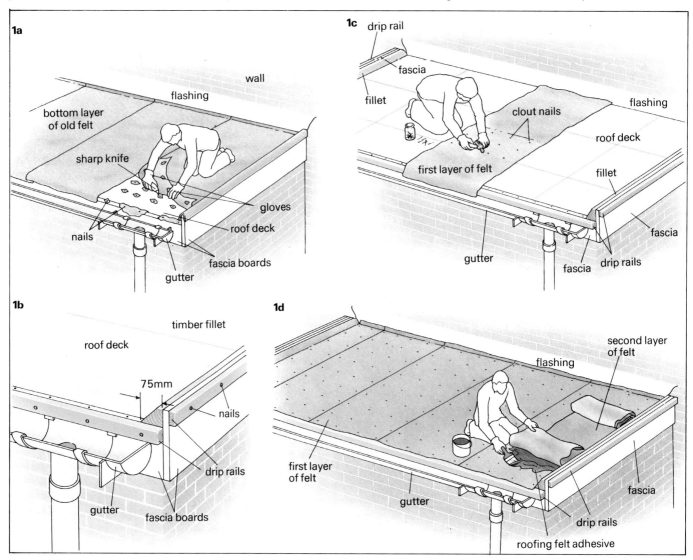

1a wall, flashing, bottom layer of old felt, sharp knife, gloves, roof deck, nails, fascia boards, gutter

1c drip rail, fascia, fillet, clout nails, flashing, roof deck, first layer of felt, fillet, gutter, fascia, drip rails, fascia

1b timber fillet, roof deck, 75mm, nails, drip rails, gutter, fascia boards

1d flashing, second layer of felt, first layer of felt, gutter, fascia, drip rails, roofing felt adhesive

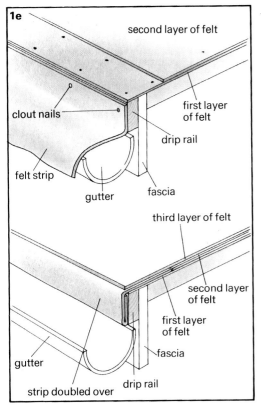

1e

second layer of felt

clout nails

felt strip

first layer of felt

drip rail

gutter

fascia

third layer of felt

second layer of felt

first layer of felt

fascia

gutter

strip doubled over

drip rail

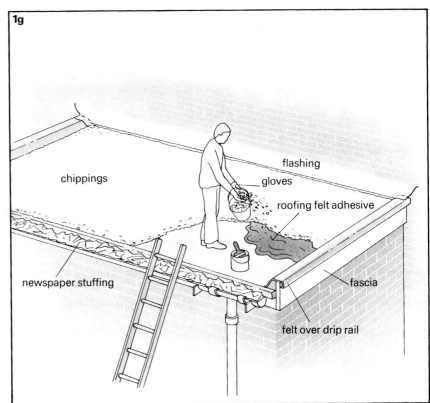

1g

chippings

flashing

gloves

roofing felt adhesive

newspaper stuffing

fascia

felt over drip rail

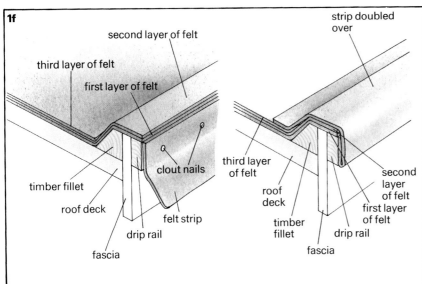

1f

second layer of felt

third layer of felt

first layer of felt

strip doubled over

timber fillet

roof deck

clout nails

drip rail

felt strip

fascia

third layer of felt

roof deck

timber fillet

second layer of felt

first layer of felt

drip rail

fascia

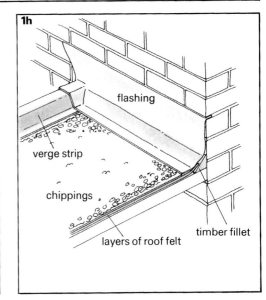

1h

flashing

verge strip

chippings

layers of roof felt

timber fillet

covering, such as severe cracks, loose areas and bad wrinkles, the roof should be stripped and the covering replaced. In the case of an asphalt roof, this work should be left to a professional. Where a concrete roof has cracked, trowel on a mortar mix to fill the cracks before treating with bitumen proofing. Where the roof has a timber base, check the timber is sound and remove and replace any unsound boards before carrying out further repairs.
Roofing felt Flat roofs covered with bituminous roofing felt are quite easy to strip and replace. On house extension or garage roofs there are usually three layers of felt fixed down over a roof deck of timber boards or chipboard sheets. Tear off the old felt, using a sharp knife to cut round the nails. It is best to wear tough gloves when doing this job since the felt is rough and may cut or scratch your hands. Remove the old fixing nails with a claw hammer or hammer them as flush with the

surface as possible. Sweep the surface clean and check it is smooth – high points can be taken off with an abrasive disc fitted to an electric drill and depressions levelled with an exterior grade filler. Nail a 50 × 38mm (2 × 1½in) batten along the outside edge or verge of the roof to serve as a drip rail over which felt will later be fixed to form an apron; this weatherproofs the edge of the roof and throws water clear of the walls of the building or into a gutter, if one is fitted. If the fascia board projects upwards at the verge, you should also nail a 75mm (3in) wide angled timber fillet behind the fascia.

Before you buy felt, consult your local building inspector to check that the type you have in mind complies with the current Building Regulations. Felt manufacturers make recommendations regarding the kind of felt to be fitted to suit the type of roof and will supply comprehensive fixing instructions. Where possible, cut the felt roughly to length and

1e At the eaves, nail a strip of felt to the drip rail and then double it back over to lie flush with the second layer of felt
1f At the verge, nail a strip of felt to the drip rail and then double it back to lap over the third layer of felt
1g Apply adhesive and chippings to the top layer of felt after stuffing the gutter with newspaper
1h At the parapet wall, fit a felt flashing with the end cut at 45 degrees and the top tucked into the raked-out mortar joint

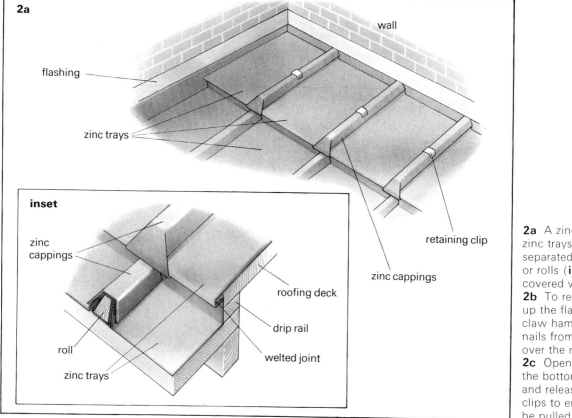

2a

wall

flashing

zinc trays

retaining clip

zinc cappings

inset

zinc cappings

roll

zinc trays

roofing deck

drip rail

welted joint

2a A zinc roof is made up of zinc trays, which are separated by timber battens or rolls (**inset**); these are covered with zinc cappings
2b To remove a tray, lever up the flashing and use a claw hammer to remove the nails from the zinc cappings over the rolls
2c Open the welted joint at the bottom edge of the tray and release the retaining clips to enable the tray to be pulled out

leave it flat for at least 24 hours before fixing to minimize the effects of subsequent curling and stretching. Usually, you will have to fix the first layer of felt to the roof boards with galvanized clout nails at 150mm (6in) intervals. Fix from the centre of the sheet outwards to prevent wrinkles and bubbles forming and secure subsequent layers of felt by brushing on roofing felt adhesive. Also apply roofing felt adhesive over the surface of the top layer of felt and sprinkle on small stone chippings to protect the felt and give a non-slip surface – or you can spread on a special chipping compound. Protect the gutter from the chippings by blocking it with newspaper or rags while you are carrying out this operation. To form the weatherproofing apron at the eaves, the middle layer of felt should be cut a little shorter than the other layers; cut a separate strip, nail it to the drip rail with galvanized clout nails and double the edge over to lie flush with, and butting against, the second layer. At the verge, a similar piece of felt is nailed to the drip rail and doubled over to form the apron and then taken over the roof to overlap the top layer of felt.

Zinc roofing Normally a zinc roof is constructed in tiers called drips and each drip is subdivided into sections or zinc trays; the trays are separated by timber battens or rolls which are also covered with zinc. While extensive repairs are probably best left to a roofing specialist, you can replace a damaged tray yourself. Where the tray meets a retaining wall there will be a flashing overlapping the tray. Lever this up and use a claw hammer or pincers to remove the nails from the zinc capping covering the rolls. Open the welted joint at the bottom edge of the tray, release the retaining clips which hold the tray in place and slide the tray free. Use the old tray as a pattern to cut the new one to size with tin snips. Repeat for the cappings, remembering to make sure

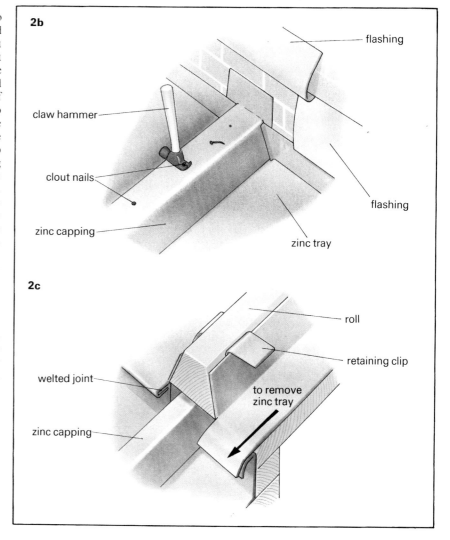

2b

flashing

claw hammer

clout nails

zinc capping

flashing

zinc tray

2c

roll

retaining clip

welted joint

zinc capping

to remove zinc tray

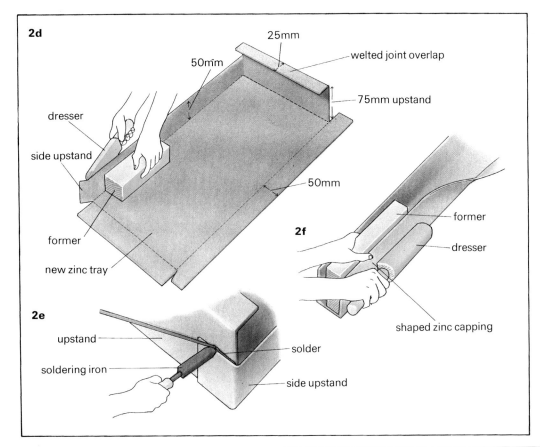

2d To shape the new tray, use a batten as a former and press the zinc up round it with a wood dresser
2e Solder the tray corners
2f Fold the new capping with a former and dresser
2g Position the new tray, butting the upturned sides against the rolls and leaving the bottom end open to form the welted joint
2h Solder the edges of the capping to the tray at the roll end

on both occasions you fold out the welted joint to cut the new zinc to the right size.

Using a batten of suitable length as a former, bend up the sides and end of the new zinc to form the upstands of the tray, clean all round with wire wool, and solder the corners. Fold the capping in the same way as the old capping. Place the new tray in position, lap the flashing over it and butt the upturned sides hard up against the rolls, folding the retaining clips over the upstands. Secure the new capping in place with galvanized nails and solder the edges of the capping at the roll end where they butt against the zinc tray underneath.

Alternatively you can strip the zinc covering and replace it with roofing felt. You can replace the zinc with metal-faced glass fibre bitumen sheeting, but this type of work is best left to a specialist.

Lead roofing Normally a lead roof should last for a long time; but if there are small damaged patches in a roof, you can solder on small pieces of lead to cover the damage. Buying sheets of lead for more extensive repair work is expensive and it is cheaper and simpler to strip off the lead and apply three layers of bituminous felt.

Shed roofs

A single sheet of mineral-surfaced roofing felt is normally used to waterproof a shed roof, but sometimes it may be covered with bitumen strip slates which simulate a tiled roof. In both cases, you can patch small tears and cracks with new pieces of roofing felt stuck down with roofing felt adhesive. If the covering is in very bad condition, it should be removed and replaced. Before carrying out replacement, remove any protruding nails with a claw hammer or drive them in flush with the roof.

Felt covering Lay new bituminous roofing felt in wide strips which run along the length of the roof. The strips should be cut and laid out for at least 24

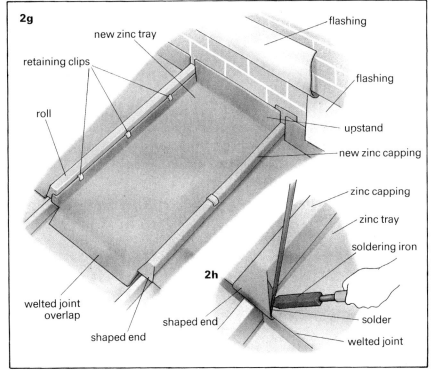

hours before fixing. Start fixing at eaves or gutter level and overlap adjacent strips by 75mm (3in), finishing off at the ridge or apex. Nail them down using 13mm ($\frac{1}{2}$in) galvanized clout nails at about 50mm (2in) intervals around the edges. Fold under exposed edges at the eaves and verges before nailing. For extra weather protection, secure the felt overlaps with roofing felt adhesive. Seal the ridge with a 300mm (or 12in) wide strip of felt fixed with adhesive and clout nails along the edges.

Bitumen strip slates These are fixed in place with galvanized clout nails. Start at the eaves and work up the roof to the ridge, making sure the strips are laid with staggered joints. With some types of strip slates, you should stick down the exposed part of each strip by melting the underside of the strip with a blowlamp: check the maker's instructions.

Corrugated roofs
Plastic, glass fibre, asbestos-cement, galvanized steel and aluminium are frequently used for corrugated roofing. In all cases, small cracks and holes can be repaired by patching with self-adhesive foil-backed flashing strip.

Patching Use a wire brush to clean the damaged area; cut the patch so it overlaps this area by at least 50mm (2in) all round and press it on. You should prime an asbestos-cement surface first with flashing strip primer to ensure the patch adheres firmly. As an alternative method, you can repair holes using the glass fibre matting repair kits sold for car bodywork repairs. When the repairs are complete, resurface the entire roof with two coats of heavy duty liquid bitumen proofing. This will seal pin-prick holes or porous areas on most surfaces, but cannot be used on thin plastic sheeting.

Replacing corrugated sheet Where there is extensive damage you should replace the damaged sheets. Use a claw hammer to remove the nails from an old sheet, then ease up the flashing and pull out the sheet. Cut the new sheet using the old sheet as a pattern. Put wood blocks under the third corrugation of a sheet next to the gap which the new sheet will fill and slide the new sheet under the raised sheet and over the sheet on the opposite side, checking it is properly in place. Remove the blocks and drill holes to take the fixing screws which should penetrate the high points of the corrugations, not the valleys. (Check with your supplier on the type of screw suitable for use with the material you are fixing.) If necessary, replace the flashing with self-adhesive flashing strip.

3a When covering a shed roof with felt, fix the first strip at the level of the eaves or gutter. Fold the felt at the corner and nail it in place (**inset**)

3b Make sure there is an overlap between adjacent strips of felt

3c Seal the ridge of the roof with a strip of felt. Where the felt laps over the edge of the ridge, fold and nail it (**inset**)

4a Use galvanized clout nails to fix trimmed bitumen strip slates at the eaves

4b Lay the rows of strips so the joints are staggered for weatherproofing

4c With some types of strip slates you will have to melt the underside of the slates with a blowtorch to stick them down

5a Use a self-adhesive flashing strip to patch small tears and cracks in corrugated roofing

5b To replace a damaged corrugated sheet, slide the new sheet under one sheet, which is raised up by a wood block, and over the sheet on the opposite side

5c Types of fixing for corrugated roofing

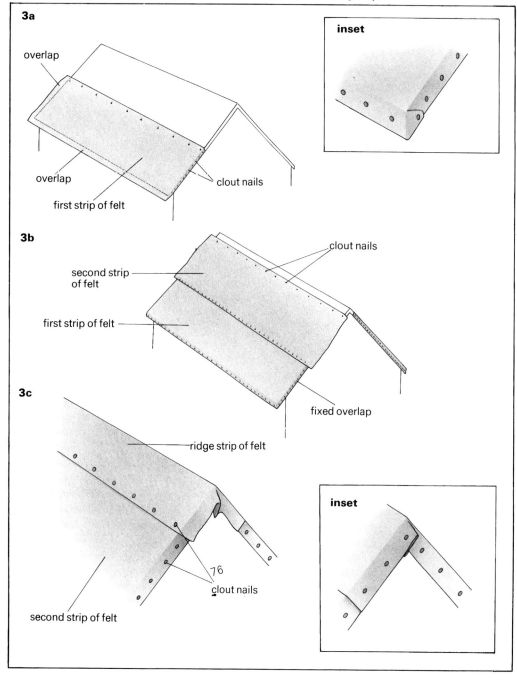

3a
overlap
overlap
clout nails
first strip of felt

inset

3b
clout nails
second strip of felt
first strip of felt
fixed overlap

3c
ridge strip of felt
clout nails
second strip of felt

inset

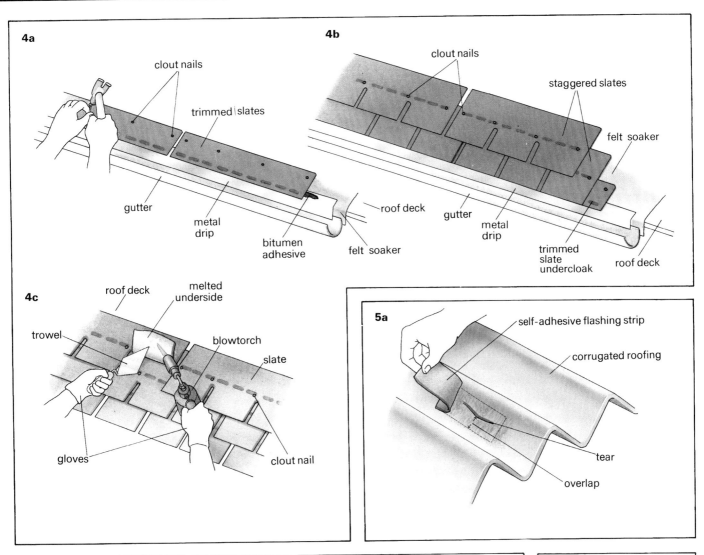

4a

clout nails

trimmed slates

gutter

metal drip

bitumen adhesive

felt soaker

roof deck

4b

clout nails

staggered slates

felt soaker

gutter

metal drip

trimmed slate undercloak

roof deck

4c

roof deck

melted underside

trowel

blowtorch

slate

gloves

clout nail

5a

self-adhesive flashing strip

corrugated roofing

tear

overlap

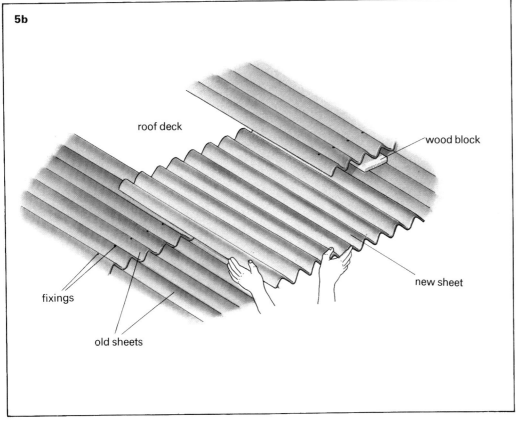

5b

roof deck

wood block

new sheet

fixings

old sheets

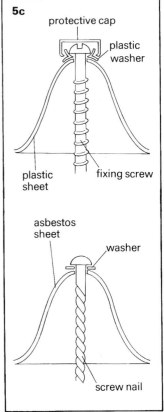

5c

protective cap

plastic washer

plastic sheet

fixing screw

asbestos sheet

washer

screw nail

Cold weather protection

If the plumbing system in your home is not adequately protected, severe weather can cause water to freeze in the pipes, producing blockages and burst pipes. You can deal with these yourself, but it is better to prevent any damage by checking your anti-frost defences every autumn.

Protecting plumbing

Frost protection is built into the structure of a well-designed, modern home and the important design points are explained below.

Service pipe This pipe conveys water from the water authority's communication pipe to the house and should be covered by at least 750mm (or 30in) of earth throughout its length. If it enters the house by a hollow, boarded floor, it should be thoroughly protected from draughts. The pipe should be taken up into the roof space – to supply the cold water storage cistern – against an internal wall.

Storage cistern The cold water storage cistern is best situated against a flue which is in constant use.

To prevent icy draughts blowing up the warning pipe leading from the cistern, you can fit a hinged copper flap over the outlet; there is, however, a risk that this will jam in the open or closed position. A better method is to extend the pipe within the cistern and bend it over so its outlet is about 38mm (1½in) below the surface of the water. There are gadgets, such as the frostguard, which make it easy to extend internally the warning pipe from a storage or flushing cistern.

The boiler, hot water storage cylinder and cold water storage cistern are best installed in a vertical column so the vulnerable cold water cistern receives the benefit of the rising warm air.

All lengths of water pipe within the roof space should be kept short and well away from the eaves.

Lagging Efficient lagging of storage tanks and pipes reduces the rate at which water loses its warmth and protects pipes exposed to cold air; but it cannot make up for a bad plumbing design and it will not add heat to the system.

Pipes to lag are those against external walls, under the ground floor and in the roof space. Don't omit the vent pipe of the hot water system since the water in this pipe is not as hot as that in the rest of the system and, if it freezes, it can create a vacuum which could damage the cylinder.

There are several types of pipe lagging available and it is best to use inorganic materials. These include wrap-round glass fibre; moulded polystyrene (which comes in rigid sections which fit round the pipe) and flexible moulded foam plastic (which you split open to fit round the pipe). Polystyrene is rather awkward to use, but is good for underground pipes since it does not absorb water. The moulded types of lagging come in a variety of sizes to fit different pipes, so make sure you buy the appropriate size.

Whichever type you use, make sure you lag behind pipes against external walls to protect them from the cold wall. Cover the tails of ball valves and all but the handles of stopcocks and gate valves; if you are using rigid lagging sections, you will need some of the wrap-round type for these areas.

Bind wrap-round insulation round the pipe like a bandage, overlapping it to prevent gaps, and secure it with string or adhesive tape. Where a pipe joins a cistern, make a full turn and tie it to hold the end in place. When joining two lengths overlap them and tie securely.

Secure moulded sections with plastic adhesive tape, starting at the cistern. Where the sections join along a length of pipe, seal the joint with tape. Open up flexible moulding along one side, slip it round the pipe and seal the opening with adhesive tape, taking particular care at any elbows. If you lag the pipes before fitting them, there is of course no need to slit the lagging; you can slide the pipe length through it. Where pipes go through a wall, make sure the insulation goes right up to the wall.

You also need to protect the cold water cistern. The easiest way to cover a square cistern is to use expanded polystyrene slabs. For a circular cistern use glass fibre tank wrap. If you have insulating material between the floor joists in the loft, make sure the area immediately below the tank is left uncovered so warm air is allowed to reach the tank.

Dealing with frozen pipes

If, in spite of your precautions, a freeze-up does occur, it is essential to deal with it immediately. If there is any delay the plug of ice will spread along the pipe and increase the risk of damage.

You can gauge the position of the freeze-up from the situation of the plumbing fittings which have stopped working. If, for instance, water is not flowing into the main cold water storage cistern but is running from the cold tap over the kitchen sink, the plug of ice must be in the rising main between the branch to the kitchen sink and the cistern.

Strip off the lagging from the affected pipe and apply heat – either with cloths soaked in hot water and wrung dry or a filled hot water bottle. If a pipe is inaccessible, direct a jet of warm air towards it from a hair dryer or the outlet of a vacuum cleaner. Fortunately modern copper tubing conducts very well and a small plug of ice can often be melted by applying heat to the pipe about a metre from the actual location of the ice.

Burst pipe If the freeze-up results in a burst pipe the first indication will probably be water dripping through a ceiling, since pipes in the loft are most likely to burst; wherever the leak, immediate action is vital. Turn off the main stopcock and open up every tap in the house. This will drain the cistern and pipes and reduce the damage. When the system is completely drained, find the position of the leak.

Damaged copper piping If you have copper piping, you will probably find a compression or soldered capillary joint will have been forced open by the expansion of ice. All you need to do in this case is fit a new joint. Copper piping does sometimes split under pressure. If that happens, you will have to cut out the defective length and insert a new length. An easy way of doing this is to insert a repair coupling.

Cut out the damaged section of pipe with a fine tooth hacksaw, leaving a gap of not more than 89mm (3½in) between the pipe ends. Remove the burr from the tube ends with a small file. One end of the coupling has a tube stop, the other is free to

Right Efficient lagging will protect pipes against freezing conditions

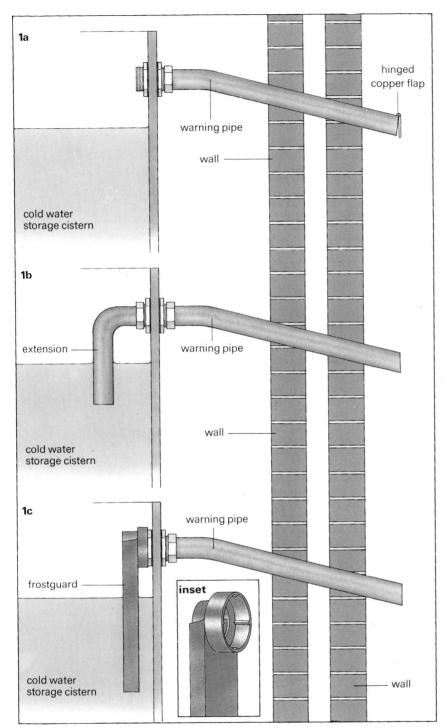

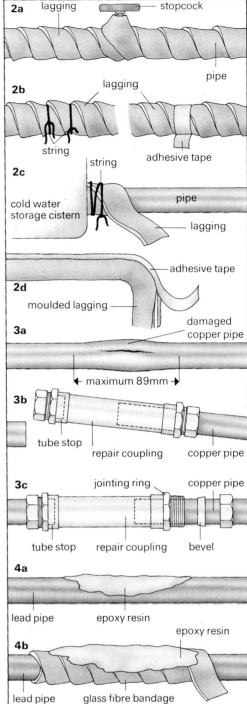

1a-c Ways of protecting cold water cistern from severe external conditions. **2a** Lagging pipe but leaving handle of stopcock clear; **2b** Secure lagging with tape or string; **2c** Where pipe meets cistern, make full turn and bind lagging firmly; **2d** Cut moulded lagging along one side, place round pipe and seal join with tape. **3a-c** Removing damaged section of copper pipe and fitting repair coupling. **4a-b** Making temporary repair to lead pipe with epoxy resin and bandage

slide along the pipe. Slacken the nuts of the coupling, spring one end of the pipe out just enough to allow you to slide the repair coupling over it. Line it up with the other pipe end and push the coupling on to it until the tube stop is reached. Unscrew the nuts and slide them and the copper jointing rings along the pipe. Apply jointing compound or gloss paint into the bevels of the fitting and around the leading edge of the jointing rings. Tighten the nuts with a spanner so the tube is lightly gripped; make another turn, or a turn and a quarter, making sure you do not overtighten.

Burst lead pipe The orthodox and approved method of repairing a burst lead pipe is to cut out the affected length and replace it with a new length of pipe; this job is best left to an expert.

You can, however, make a temporary repair with

one of the epoxy resin repair kits available. Dry the affected length of pipe thoroughly and knock the edges of the split together with a hammer. Rub down with abrasive paper. Make up the resin filler according to the manufacturer's instructions and apply it round the pipe to cover the split and the surrounding area. While the filler is still plastic, bind round it with a glass fibre bandage and 'butter' a further layer of resin filler over the bandage. When thoroughly set, rub down with abrasive paper to make an unobtrusive joint. You will be able to use the pipe again within a few hours.

Frost and the hot water system

A well designed hot water cylinder storage system provides any home with its best insurance against the risk of frost damage. No matter how effectively a cylinder is lagged, some warmth will always be conducted along the pipework and rise up into the roof space, giving a measure of protection to the cold water storage cistern. This again emphasizes the importance of having the cold water storage cistern sited directly above the hot water cylinder – and not insulating the area immediately below the cistern.

A packaged plumbing system, in which the storage cistern and hot water cylinder are combined in one unit, gives virtually total protection to the cistern and the pipes in the immediate vicinity as long as the water in the cylinder is hot.

Boiler explosion

One of the great fears, particularly where water is heated by means of a boiler, is still that of a boiler explosion – and people often worry a great deal more about their hot water system during cold spells than they do about the cold water supply pipes. However, if you can understand the cause of boiler explosions and take simple and straightforward precautions to avoid them, you need never have a moment's anxiety over this happening.

A cylinder hot water system is, in effect, a large 'U' shape tube with the boiler at its base and the vent pipe and open storage cistern providing the two open ends. Provided the pipe run between the boiler and the vent pipe – or the boiler and the cold water storage cistern – is not obstructed, there can be no dangerous build-up of pressure. A spring-loaded safety valve, positioned on either the flow or return pipe in the immediate vicinity of the boiler, provides a final line of defence.

Boiler explosions usually take place when a house is reoccupied after having been empty during a prolonged spell of severe weather. The existence of the normal protective measure – lagging – will not add warmth to the plumbing system; all it can do is slow down the rate of heat loss. While the house is occupied, this is all that is needed; the fabric of the house is warm and water is constantly being drawn off and replaced. When the house is empty, however, the fabric chills off and water stagnates in the supply and distribution pipes. If a spell of cold weather intervenes, a severe freeze-up is inevitable. Plugs of ice will form in the upper part of the vent pipe and in the cold water supply pipe from the cistern to the cylinder. Ice may even form in the boiler itself and in the pipes between the boiler and the cylinder.

The real danger comes if, under these circumstances, the boiler fire is lit. Water in the boiler will heat up, but it will not be able to circulate or expand. Internal pressure will build up until, ultimately, something gives and releases it. In an instant the superheated water in the boiler will turn into steam, with many thousand times the volume of the water from which it was formed, and the boiler will explode like a bomb – with equally devastating results.

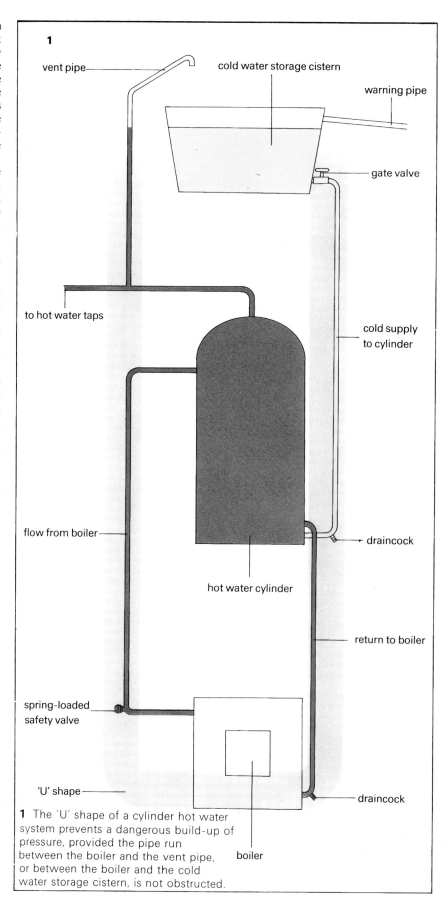

1 The 'U' shape of a cylinder hot water system prevents a dangerous build-up of pressure, provided the pipe run between the boiler and the vent pipe, or between the boiler and the cold water storage cistern, is not obstructed.

Cylinder implosion

Boiler explosions are, happily, an extremely rare occurrence. Cylinder implosion – or collapse – is rather more common in frosty weather; this is particularly likely to occur when the boiler is allowed to go out at night. Small plugs of ice form in the upper part of the vent pipe and in the upper part of the cold water supply pipe to the cylinder. The warm water in the cylinder and boiler cools and contracts, producing a partial vacuum. Cylinders are not constructed to withstand external pressure and, when this occurs, the storage cylinder will collapse like a paper bag under the weight of atmospheric pressure.

The way to avoid either cylinder collapse or boiler explosion is to keep the boiler fire alight and the house warm during cold weather, although this may be difficult if you have to go away for any length of time.

Useful precautions

If you have a reliable automatic central heating system, the best precaution is to leave it turned on at a low setting or under the control of a 'frost-stat'. Keep internal doors open to allow warm air to circulate through the house and partially remove the flap to the loft space to permit some warmth to penetrate to this area as well.

You may not be able to control your central heating system in this way; but both it and the primary circuit of your indirect hot water system can be protected by the addition of a proprietary anti-freeze solution. Don't, however, be tempted to use the same anti-freeze you put in your car radiator, since it is quite unsuitable for central heating systems.

The only other really safe precaution is to drain the domestic hot and cold water systems. Turn off the main stopcock (located where the mains water enters the house) and empty the system by opening the draincock immediately above it if there is one. Remember to attach a length of hose and run it to the sink or outside, otherwise you will flood the room. Open all the taps as well until water stops running. The hot water storage cylinder and – with a direct hot water system – the boiler will still be filled with water. With a direct system this can be drained by connecting one end of a length of hose to the draincock beside the boiler and taking the other end to the sink (if nearby) or outside. Open the draincock and wait while the boiler empties. If you have an indirect hot water system – or a direct system heated only by an immersion heater – the appropriate draincock will be located by the cylinder, probably at the base of the cold water supply pipe which feeds it.

When you return home, remember the system is empty – and make sure you refill it before lighting the boiler fire. To reduce the risk of air locks forming as you do this, connect one end of a length of hose to the cold tap over the kitchen sink and the other end to the boiler draincock. Open up the tap and the draincock and the system will fill upwards, driving air before it.

2 A spring-loaded safety valve will give extra protection to your hot water system. If pressure builds up, the safety valve opens and relieves pressure in the pipes. Before fitting a safety valve, bind it with PTFE thread sealing tape
3 Wiring a frost-stat into an automatic central heating system. For a programmer with separate hot water and central heating settings, you will need a double pole frost-stat as shown in the diagram. The programmer selector should be set to 'Off' when the frost-stat is to be used

3

flow or return
pipe near boiler

compression tee

safety valve

4

Warning Always remember to switch off the immersion heater before you drain the system.

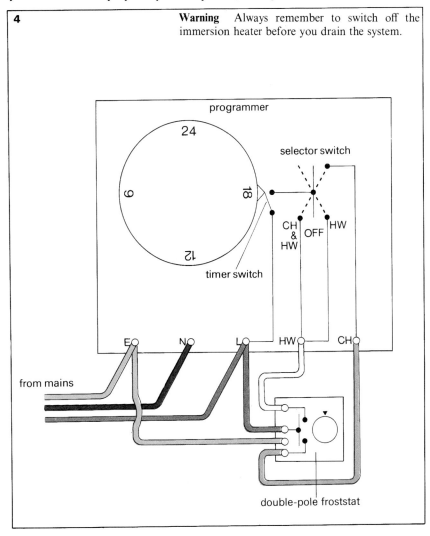

programmer

24

9

18

12

selector switch

CH
&
HW

OFF

HW

timer switch

E   N   L   HW   CH

from mains

double-pole fr018stat

Insulating the loft

Heating costs rise with the warm air if heat is allowed to escape through the roof. By insulating the loft area you can keep down the bills and hold heat where it belongs – in the house. This is a job well within the scope of the handyman, requiring no special techniques. The materials are all readily available.

A loft that has no insulation will account for a heat loss of about 25 per cent in the average size house. Several forms of insulation are available and fall into two categories: loose-fill materials such as vermiculite granules, and the blanket type made from glass fibre or mineral wool. The materials we mention are all resistant to fire and you must check on the fire-resistance of any alternative product you consider buying. As a precaution, first treat all timber for woodworm.

joists in most houses, and can be cut quite easily with a large pair of scissors or a sharp knife. Even handled carefully, glass fibre can irritate the skin, so always wear gloves when working with it.

Mineral wool Another blanket insulation material, this is made from spun molten rock and is handled in the same way as glass fibre.

Laying rolls Place the roll of material between the joists and tuck the end under the eaves. Working backwards, unroll the material until you reach the other end of the roof. Cut it and tuck the end under the eaves as before. Lay the strip flat between the joists or, if it is a little wider, turn the sides up against the sides of the joists. Continue in this way until the whole loft area has been covered. If you have to join two strips in the middle of the roof, overlap them by about 75mm (3in).

Below left To lay granules, pour them between joists and level them with T-shaped piece of timber
Below If your insulating roll is wider than space between joists, turn up each side against joists
Below centre Don't lay insulation under cold water cistern; leave area uncovered so warm air from below can stop water freezing
Bottom Use latex adhesive to glue piece of glass fibre on loft flap

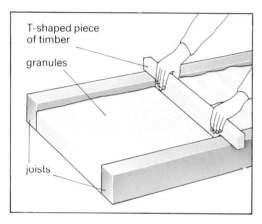

Granule insulation
One advantage of using granules to insulate your loft is that they flow easily and smoothly and will fill any awkward spaces. They are also safe to handle since they do not contain any splinters or loose fibres.

Vermiculite Expanded mica in granule form, this is supplied in easy-to-handle bags. The manufacturer's instructions will give you a guide to the number of bags needed for specific areas.

You should wear a mask and some form of eye protection when using vermiculite since it is a dusty material that easily gets into the atmosphere.

Laying granules Pour vermiculite between the joists to a depth of about 125mm (5in), which will bring it almost level with the top of the joists in most lofts. Level the granules by drawing a piece of timber along the top edges of the joists. If the joists are significantly deeper than 125mm, level the granules to the required depth by dragging a T-shaped spreader along the top of the joists. Make this from any piece of scrap wood a little longer than the joist separation, and notch its corners so the base of the T will fit between the joists.

Blanket insulation
This form of insulation does not need to be laid as thickly as granules and should be used in lofts where there are gaps around the eaves, since wind might blow the granules about.

Glass fibre The most economical form of blanket insulation for loft spaces. It comes in 100 or 150mm (4 or 6in) thick rolls and is available in 400mm (16in) widths, equivalent to the space between roof

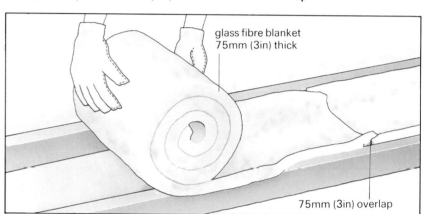

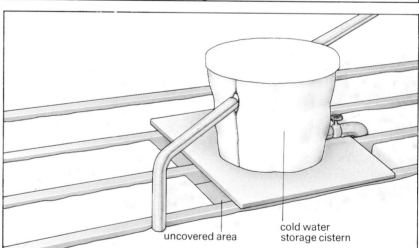

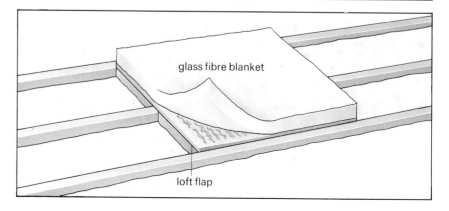

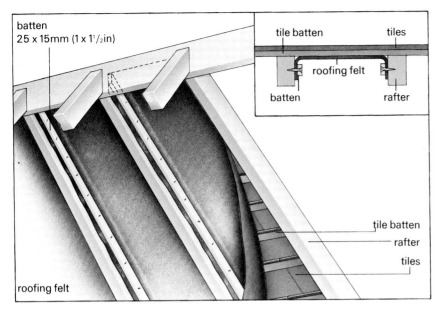

batten
25 x 15mm (1 x 1¹/₂in)

tile batten   tiles

roofing felt

batten   rafter

tile batten

rafter

tiles

roofing felt

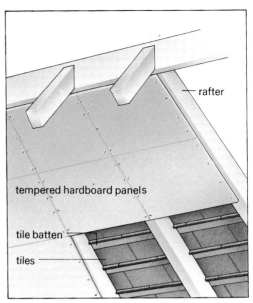

rafter

tempered hardboard panels

tile batten

tiles

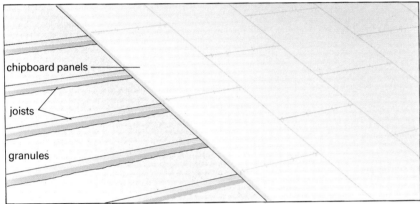

chipboard panels

joists

granules

Top When fixing felt between rafters, allow enough width to turn onto rafters and hold felt in place by screwing through battens and felt into rafters. **Inset** Cross-section of felt and batten fixing

Top right When insulating with tempered hardboard, butt-join panels and fix to rafters with countersunk screws

Above Improve insulation by laying floor using chipboard panels, staggering joins and screwing through sides of each panel into joists. Cut panels so they butt-join each other in middle of each joist

Insulating awkward areas You will find it easier to cover awkwardly shaped or inaccessible areas with granules. A 125mm (5in) thickness of granules is roughly equivalent to 100mm (4in) of blanket material in terms of insulation efficiency.

Warning Whichever method of insulation you use, don't insulate under the cold water tank. You must allow a warm air current to flow from below to prevent the tank from freezing in cold weather. But don't forget to insulate the loft flap or cover. Cut a piece of blanket material to the size of the cover and stick it down with a latex adhesive. And when working in the loft, remember to tread only on the joists or on a board placed across them.

Other forms of insulation

Even more insulation can be provided if you make a floor to the loft by fixing panels of chipboard or planks of timber to the joists above the insulating material. This will also give you extra storage space, but you may have to strengthen the joists by spanning the load-bearing walls with large timbers before laying the floor if you want to put heavy items on it. Seek advice from a builder or your local authority.

Heat loss through the roof space can be further reduced by lining the ceilings immediately below the loft with an insulating-type material such as expanded polystyrene or acoustic tiles. It should be emphasized, however, that this is not a substitute for loft insulation.

Effective insulation of the floor will make the loft colder, so it is vitally important to ensure the

cold water tank (except beneath it) and all pipes are thoroughly protected, otherwise they will be susceptible to frost damage.

Protection from frost

The type of loft most likely to suffer from frost damage is one with an unboarded tile-hung roof. If your roof has no close-boarding or roofing felt – as is the case with many older houses – it is worth insulating it.

Cut lengths of roofing felt about 200mm (8in) wider than the distance between the rafters. Lay one long edge onto the inside edge of one rafter, lay a 25 × 15mm (1 × ½in) batten onto the felt and screw through the batten and felt into the rafter. Use No 8 countersunk screws 25mm long, spacing them at 300–380mm (12–15in) intervals. Don't use nails as the vibration from hammering could dislodge and break the roof tiles. Stretch the roof felt across to the next rafter and fix the other edge onto the edge of that rafter, again screwing through a batten. Leave a space between the roof and the felt to allow air to circulate, otherwise you may find rot will form on the rafters.

An alternative to roofing felt is tempered hardboard: butt-joint each panel of hardboard to the next by screwing it to the centre of each rafter with No 8 countersunk screws 25mm long. You may have to trim your cut panels so they fit neatly in the middle of each rafter.

All this work can be done in easy stages; when you have finished, the roof space will certainly remain warmer in winter and will also be much cleaner – an important consideration if you are using the loft for storage.

Cutting sheets to size

Boards are available in 2440 × 1830mm (8 × 6ft) and 1830 × 1220mm (6 × 4ft) sheets. You need 25mm (1in) thick flooring grade chipboard or 6mm (¼in) thick hardboard. Cut the larger sheet into six convenient 1830 × 407mm (6ft × 1ft 4in) panels, or the smaller one into three panels of the same size. If the loft opening space allows, cut the larger sheet into three 1830 × 813mm (6ft × 2ft 8in) panels, or the smaller sheet into one similar size panel and one 1830 × 407mm (6ft × 1ft 4in) panel.

Door, floor and window insulation

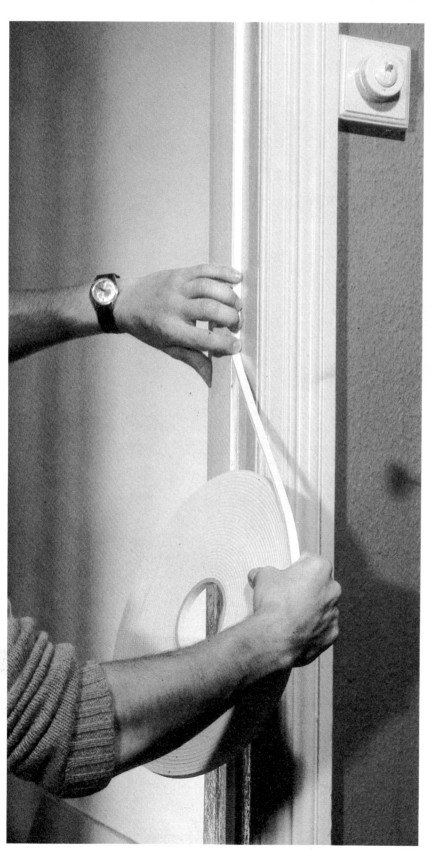

Cold air leaking in through gaps around doors and windows or through floorboards can account for up to ten per cent of the heat lost from a house. Eliminating the worst effects of draughts through doors, floors and windows is quite a simple task for the handyman, giving immediate financial returns which quickly pay for the inexpensive materials. Your winters will also be considerably more comfortable in a draught-free home. One solution to prevent draughts and help keep up the inside heat is to fit an excluder.

Draught excluders
One of the cheapest draught excluders is the plastic foam strip with an adhesive backing which you peel off as you apply the strip to a clean surface and cut to length with scissors. Although this is simple to use, it is less durable than other types and has to be replaced each year. It is effective if the gaps are not too wide and two strips can be used, for instance, on doors and door jambs or windows and frames so they come together when the door or window is closed.

Two more permanent draught excluders are the plastic (polypropylene) strip and the sprung metal strip. Both of these have ready-punched clearance holes, usually at about 25mm (1in) intervals, are tacked round the door or window rebate and are not visible when the door is closed. Because closing the door puts the strip under tension, however, it can cause the door to stick.

When using aluminium or phosphor bronze strips, position them with care and make sure there are no kinks when nailing them into place. For metal windows you should use an aluminium strip with a special groove to fit the window frame. Clean the frame with a stiff wire brush to remove rust and dirt and fill pit holes with plastic filler before applying the strip. If you clean right down to the bare metal you will have to apply a coat of metal primer after filling holes and leave it to dry before fixing the strip. With wire cutters or scissors, cut the strip in sections to the size of the frame sides and mitre across the width at the ends of each section. Fitting the top piece first and then the sides and bottom, push the groove of the strip over the outside lip of the frame. Push the corner clip tongues over the strip junctions and then turn the tongues of the clips over the flanges to secure the strip.

Under-door draughts
To eliminate draughts under doors, you can nail or screw a piece of 6mm ($\frac{1}{4}$in) thick timber batten at regular intervals, say two nails or screws per floorboard, across the threshold to form an effective seal. A carpet of the same thickness placed either side of the batten will stop people tripping

Foam tape seal, impregnated with adhesive, comes in 5 or 20m (16 or 65ft) long rolls. Easy to apply, it can be painted; and because it is very flexible you do not have to mitre the corners

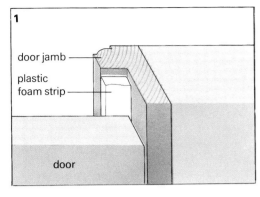

1

door jamb

plastic
foam strip

door

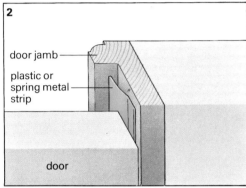

2

door jamb

plastic or
spring metal
strip

door

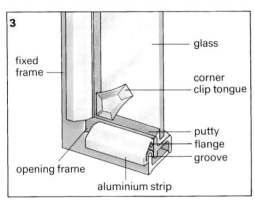

3

fixed
frame

glass

corner
clip tongue

putty
flange
groove

opening frame

aluminium strip

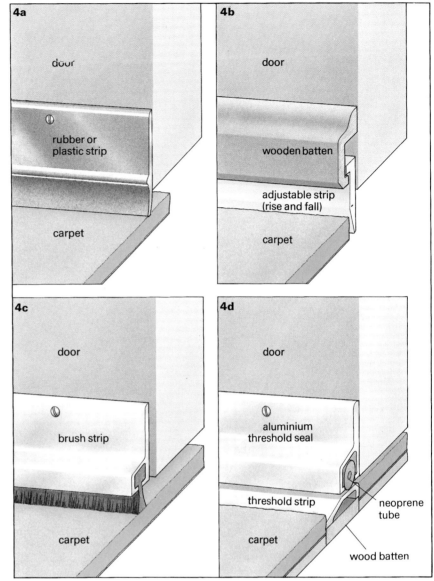

4a

door

rubber or
plastic strip

carpet

4b

door

wooden batten

adjustable strip
(rise and fall)

carpet

4c

door

brush strip

carpet

4d

door

aluminium
threshold seal

threshold strip

neoprene
tube

carpet

wood batten

For doors and windows
excluder (of type required)
tacks, nails, screws, adhesive (as needed)
wire-cutters or tin snips
scissors
hammer
hacksaw (for aluminium)
panel saw (for wood)
screwdriver
plane (as needed)
wire brush (as needed)
plastic filler (as needed)
metal primer (as needed)

For floors
papier mâché or wood filler
22mm ($\frac{7}{8}$in) quadrant or scotia moulding
32mm ($1\frac{1}{4}$in) oval wire nails
paper-faced glass fibre flanged
    building roll
knife
staple gun
staples
hammer
filling knife

equipment

over it. Alternatively, bevel the edges of the batten with a plane to make a less sharp rise from the floor.

Other excluders are made of rubber mouldings, aluminium sections or a combination of metal and plastic, so you must choose the most effective for the job in hand.

Warning You may have to take the door off its hinges and trim the bottom so the door opens and shuts freely. Otherwise, fix excluders when the door is in place.

A simple type of excluder for interior doors is a flexible plastic or rubber strip which you screw or stick to the bottom of the door so it brushes over the floor covering. Measure carefully so you do not fix this too high to be effective or too low so as to put too much wear on the floor covering. If the door has to clear a mat, a rise and fall type excluder is available. Here a flexible strip is forced, by moving over the floor covering, to ride up into a hollow wood moulding fitted to the bottom of the door and drops back into place when the door is shut. A brush strip excluder and aluminium threshold seal are also designed to ride over carpets. For exterior doors some draught excluder threshold strips come in two halves – one is fixed to the threshold and the other to the door. The two halves interlock when the door is closed.

1 Plastic foam strip attached to door jamb
2 Plastic or sprung metal strip fixed to door jamb
3 Aluminium strip around window frame
4a Flexible rubber or plastic strip on bottom of door
4b Rise and fall strip
4c Brush strip attached to metal plate at bottom of door to ride over carpet
4d Aluminium threshold seal with threshold strip raised to clear carpet

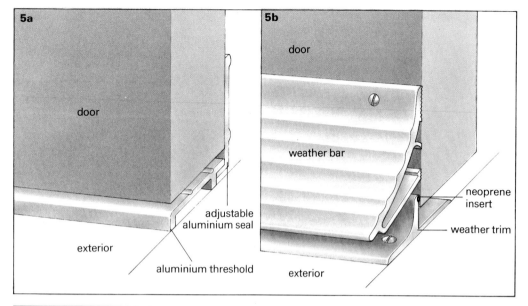

5a door

adjustable
aluminium seal

exterior

aluminium threshold

5b door

weather bar

neoprene
insert

weather trim

exterior

5a Aluminium door strip in
two halves which interlock
5b Weatherproof threshold
excluder

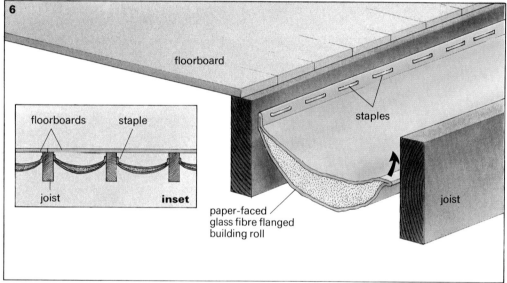

6

floorboard

staples

floorboards   staple

joist   **inset**

joist

paper-faced
glass fibre flanged
building roll

6 Paper-faced glass fibre
flanged building roll stapled
between joists. **Inset** Staple
to each joist in turn to
insulate complete floor

A badly-fitting letter-box can be very draughty.
Inexpensive draught excluders are made specifically
to overcome this problem.

Floor draughts

Having prevented draughts around doors and
windows, the problem may still not have been
entirely solved. Floorboards may have gaps which
you should plug with papier-mâché or wood filler.
You can also nail down strips of quadrant or scotia
moulding to the floor to cover gaps between the
floor and the skirting. Covering the floor with either
vinyl or carpet afterwards makes an even better job.

If the boards are badly worn and damaged, and
there are a lot of gaps between them, it is best to
relay the floor. If it is a ground-floor room this is a
good opportunity to install underfloor insulation.
Underfloor insulation A very simple method is to
staple paper-faced, glass-fibre, flanged building
roll under the floorboards. Rolls are available in a
range of widths to fit exactly between the joists.

Using a staple gun or hammer and staples, fix
one flange of the roll to a joist. The staples should
be about 100mm (4in) apart. Then staple the flange
on the other side of the roll to the next joist and
repeat the process for the other joists to complete
the insulation.

Checking for draughts

It is best to work systematically around the house
so no likely areas are missed. Eliminate the worst
draughts first. To find out where door and window
draughts are coming from, check paintwork which
has not been washed down for some time. Draughts
bring with them a considerable amount of dirt, so
a build-up of dirt around the edges of doors and
windows and their frames indicates some form of
excluder is needed. Another way is to hold a lighted
candle a safe distance away from the edges of doors
and windows and move it gently along the line of
the edge. Any sudden flickering of the flame indicates a draught. Don't get too close to any soft
furnishings when using this method.

Double-glazing

Undoubtedly, this is the best answer to a draughty
window and double-glazing will be covered in
detail later on in the book. A well-fitting system
will completely seal off the sources of entry of cold
air. Although this is certainly an expensive under-
taking solely to overcome draughts, remember that
not only will sound insulation be substantially
increased, but additionally a quite considerable
saving on fuel bills will result after the initial
outlay.

Wall insulation

Heat loss through walls can be reduced in a number of ways. Apart from one specialist method, there are three simple jobs you can tackle yourself – lining walls with plasterboard laminate, expanded polystyrene or foil.

Heat produced in a house eventually escapes to the outside via draughts and through the roof, walls and windows. The nature of the building affects the rate of loss and the path it takes. A bungalow loses more heat through the roof, while a two-storey detached house loses more through the walls. After thermal insulation there will still be heat losses, but the warmth will be dissipated at a much slower rate and heat can therefore be replaced at an equally slower rate. If your heating system is inadequate, insulation can at least ensure more effective use of the heat before it escapes.

Besides comfort from warmth, another reason for insulation is to reduce condensation. The warmer the air in a heated room, the more water vapour it can contain. When the air cools, as it does when it meets a colder wall or window, the water turns into droplets known as condensation. Insulating the walls results in these internal surfaces being kept warmer and the heat in the room being retained longer, so there is not such a dramatic contrast between the temperature of the air and the surfaces on which condensation forms. So condensation is eliminated or at least reduced. Also, insulation means that heating levels can be kept lower and, when desirable, temperatures can be boosted more effectively.

Cavity walls

Insulation of cavity walls is not a job for the home handyman – it should be carried out only by an approved contractor. The material generally used for cavity filling is urea formaldehyde foam which is injected into the cavity under pressure through holes drilled in the outer wall. There it sets, trapping millions of tiny air pockets which act as a barrier against escaping heat.

Other materials used are mineral wool fibre blown into the cavity in a similar way to urea

To insulate cavity walls, small holes are drilled in the mortar courses (below), the foam is pumped into the cavity (top) and the holes made good (above)

formaldehyde foam, and glass fibre panels placed in the cavity at the time the wall is built.

Warning Installing cavity wall insulation requires Building Regulations approval from your local authority. The materials and methods used must be approved, especially if urea-formaldehyde foam types are being installed.

Solid walls

There are a number of ways to insulate solid walls. The method you choose will depend on the lengths you wish to go to and the time and money you have available.

Lining with boards
One of the most common and effective methods of insulating solid walls is to line the inside of exterior walls with insulating board. Good results can be obtained with ordinary fibre insulating panels, but greater savings in heat loss can be gained by using plasterboard laminate, which is an extremely bad conductor of heat. This material consists of rigid urethane foam (polyurethane having a very low level of thermal conductivity) with a tough waterproof backing, a vapour barrier and a layer of plasterboard with a paper backing. When used on ceilings in particular, this board not only reduces heat losses and gives a surface which warms up rapidly but, when bonded to the ceiling with adhesive and finished with gypsum plaster or texturing compound, it minimises the risk of condensation and is especially valuable in combating persistent condensation. For use on walls, the total thickness of board should be 21mm (or $\frac{7}{8}$in). It is

most effective when fixed to a timber batten framework and used with other insulating material such as mineral wool quilting.

Fixing First remove all electrical fittings (after isolating the supply at the mains), cove, window and door surrounds and skirting. Cut the boards to shape by slicing through the waterproof backing and foam with a sharp knife or fine tooth saw, before snapping the board and cutting through the facing paper. It is important to cut away the foam at the joins so plasterboard edges will butt together to give a continuous surface. With screws and wall plugs, fix a timber batten framework (treated with wood preservative) to the wall. The main framework is made of 50 × 25mm (2 × 1in) timber and the inside supporting pieces of 38 × 25mm (1½ × 1in) timber. Ensure the timber framework is 25mm (1in) thick overall. Apply impact adhesive to the wall and loosely fix strips of mineral wool quilting between the battens. Then apply impact adhesive to the battens in strips and in a corresponding position on the boards so the strips match up when the two surfaces are joined. Fix the boards in place, taking care to position them accurately since they cannot easily be moved once contact has been made. For a smooth finish, fill any gaps between the boards with cellulose filler reinforced with plasterboard joint tape.

You will have to remount electrical fittings and refix ceiling cover door and window surrounds and skirting to bring these to the new level. If desirable, window sills can be tiled to raise their level using extra tiles positioned on top of the existing sill so they project slightly in front of the face of the plasterboard.

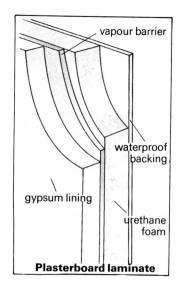

Plasterboard laminate

Above The composition of plasterboard laminate – an extremely effective insulating material
Below left To fix the boards, screw a timber framework to the walls and apply mineral wool quilting between the battens
Below Spread impact adhesive on the boards and the battens and position the boards accurately on the framework

Fixing mineral wool between battens

mineral wool

adhesive

batten

wall

skirting

Fixing plasterboard on battens

plasterboard laminate

adhesive

mineral wool

batten

skirting

adhesive on edges

adhesive to match battens

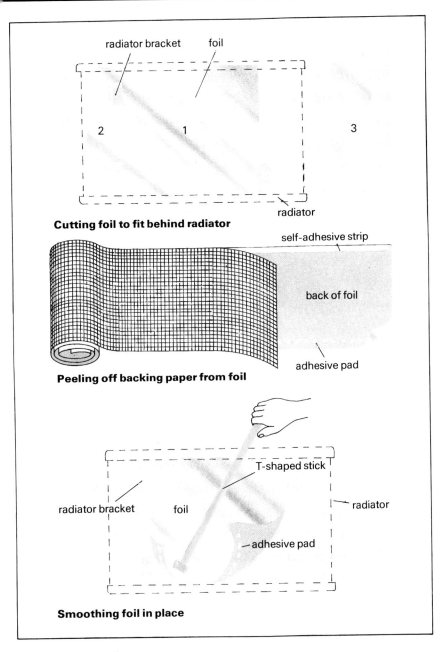

radiator bracket   foil

2   1   3

radiator

Cutting foil to fit behind radiator

self-adhesive strip

back of foil

adhesive pad

Peeling off backing paper from foil

T-shaped stick

radiator bracket   foil

radiator

adhesive pad

Smoothing foil in place

Above Use heat-reflecting foil behind radiators. Cut the foil into three, trimming it to fit round the radiator brackets. Peel off the paper backing, position the foil behind the radiator and smooth it into place

Lining behind radiators

It is also worthwhile lining the wall behind radiators with self-adhesive heat reflecting foil. This is reinforced with glass fibre and plastic-coated (to prevent tarnishing for several years).

Turn off the radiators and make sure the wall behind them is cool and clean before applying the foil. Cut the foil to a size slightly smaller than the radiator so it will not protrude when in position. For easy application, cut it into three pieces with slots in the end sections cut to fit round the radiator brackets. Remove the backing of the centre piece, place it in position against the wall and smooth it down with the applicator which is supplied with the foil. Repeat for the end pieces.

Another type of foil is available which allows more flexibility when positioning, where there is very limited space between the radiator and wall. It is fixed by an adhesive tape at the top and self-adhesive pads at the bottom. Hang the foil behind the radiator and, when it is in the correct position, press along the top to seal the tape to the wall. Then press the pads at the bottom into place to complete this very simple process for reducing heat wastage.

Both types of foil are easier to fix than the frequently-used aluminium kitchen foil, which tears easily during fixing. Applying any foil is obviously considerably simplified if access to the wall is improved by removal of the radiator from its wall brackets. If the radiators are positioned below a window, make sure no damp is penetrating the wall around the window frame before fixing foil, as the drying effect will be reduced.

Lining with expanded polystyrene

A simple, inexpensive way of reducing condensation on cold exterior walls is to line them with expanded polystyrene veneer before papering or decorating. However, these veneers are not thick enough to cut down significantly on heat losses.

This lining is available in 2–5mm (or $\frac{1}{12}$ - $\frac{3}{16}$in) thicknesses and is supplied in rolls. Apply it in the same way as wallpaper. Make sure walls are clean and dry then spread a heavy duty fungicidal wallpaper adhesive or polystyrene adhesive onto the wall and apply the lining. At joins allow 13mm ($\frac{1}{2}$in) overlap, cut the overlap with a sharp knife, remove the waste edges, apply more adhesive and lightly roll the edges. If you intend to decorate with a heavy wallpaper, it is advisable to apply a lining paper over the polystyrene lining before fixing the wallpaper.

Expanded polystyrene panels or tiles can be used instead. Use the tile-fixing adhesive recommended by the manufacturer. If you decide to paint the tiles or panels, remember to use a fire-retardant paint. Check with your supplier which paint is suitable.

Warning Never paint expanded polystyrene with gloss paint, since this can dangerously increase the rate of surface spread of flame in a fire.

Lining with plasterboard laminate
21mm (or $\frac{7}{8}$in) thick plasterboard
    laminate insulating boards
50 × 25mm (2 × 1in) timber batten
38 × 25mm (1$\frac{1}{2}$×1in) timber batten
wood preservative
No 10 countersunk screws 63mm (2$\frac{1}{2}$in)
    long, wall plugs 38mm (1$\frac{1}{2}$in) long
mineral wool quilting
additional tiles for sill (if needed)
trimming knife or fine tooth saw
hand or electric drill, 5mm ($\frac{3}{16}$ in) twist
    drill and masonry bits,
    countersink bit
impact adhesive
hammer, screwdriver
cellulose filler, plasterboard joint tape

Lining with expanded polystyrene
expanded polystyrene veneer
heavy duty fungicidal wallpaper
    adhesive or polystyrene adhesive
brush, knife, boxwood roller
lining paper (if needed)
expanded polystyrene panels or tiles,
    tile adhesive (for ceiling)

Lining behind radiators
self-adhesive heat reflecting radiator
    foil with applicator, or foil with
    self-adhesive pads and tape
scissors   **equipment**

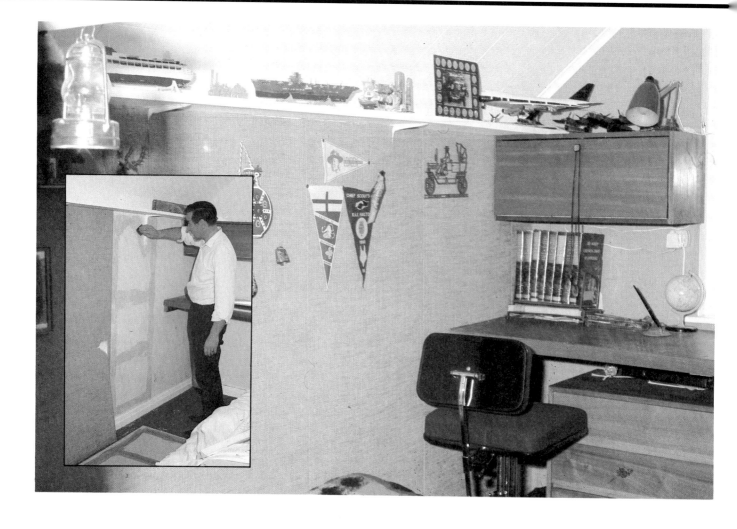

Insulating with boards

Hardboards and insulating boards are made from wood: the natural timber is reduced to fibres which are then reassembled to form large sheets. There is no grain, there are no knots and the surface is smooth and even every time. Wood fibre boards provide insulation where it's needed – on the warm side – to reduce heat loss through walls, ceilings and floors.

Types of board
The range of special types for a great variety of commercial uses is considerable, but for the home handyman the ones most readily available – apart from insulating board – are standard, tempered, medium and decorated hardboard.

Insulating board is non-compressed, lightweight and porous and is used for heat insulation, particularly on ceilings and walls. It is available in 13, 19 and 25mm ($\frac{1}{2}$, $\frac{3}{4}$ and 1in) thicknesses and also comes in the form of planks or tiles. Decorated insulating board is most commonly found in the form of ceiling tiles.

Conditioning Wood fibre boards may take up moisture from the surrounding air, causing them to expand, so it is always best to condition the boards before fixing. The treatment varies with the type of board so always check first with your supplier.

All these materials are relatively easy to handle and will cover large areas quickly. The following suggestions will give you ideas for using boards, planks and tiles.

Insulating walls
Hardboard and insulating boards can provide effective insulation if used on the inside of external walls. In houses with solid walls – as is the case with more than half of Britain's homes – this is almost the only way of providing insulation.

Where the board is unlikely to suffer rough treatment (in bedrooms, for example) and the walls are sound and flat, decorated insulating board may be stuck direct with impact adhesive. Denser standard or medium hardboards should be used if walls are likely to suffer at the hands of children. These provide heat insulation when mounted on a batten framework by creating an air gap. Lining the cavity with aluminium foil will also help.

Direct gluing Prepare painted walls by washing with household detergent or a solution of water and sugar soap. Glasspaper down to remove any flaking paint and to provide a key for the adhesive. Wallpapered areas must be completely stripped and glasspapered down.

Above Boards finished with hessian provide an attractive wall covering as well as insulation against heat loss. Fix the boards quickly by gluing them direct to the wall with impact adhesive **(inset)**

Fixing to battens (wall)

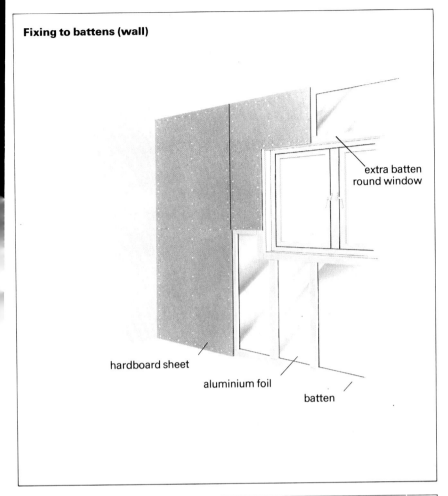

extra batten
round window

hardboard sheet

aluminium foil

batten

Order of tiling unsquare ceiling

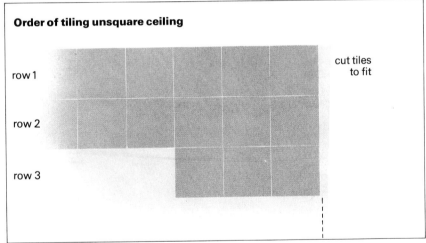

row 1

row 2

row 3

cut tiles
to fit

Spread impact adhesive in strips on both the wall and the insulating boards. Start fixing at the corner of the wall, as far as possible pressing each board onto the wall from the centre, upwards and down-'wards, to prevent bulging. Butt-join the boards, taking care not to damage the edges.

Fixing to battens Construct the framework from 50 × 25mm (2 × 1in) timber battens. Drill holes in the horizontal battens at about 400mm (16in) intervals for standard hardboards and 610mm (24in) intervals for thicker ones. Drill holes in the vertical battens at 1200mm (48in) intervals. Now drill corresponding holes in the wall, insert wall fixings and screw the battens into position. Make sure the battens are level, packing low areas with hardboard offcuts if necessary.

Fixing the boards If desired, tape sheets of aluminium foil into place between the battens. Fix decorated boards to the framework with impact adhesive to avoid damaging the finish and work from the centre of the board, upwards and downwards, to prevent the board bulging in the middle.

Other types of board should be fixed with rust-resistant round head nails or hardboard pins. Fix the top of the board to the battens about 13mm ($\frac{1}{2}$in) in from the edge at 100mm (4in) intervals, working outwards from the centre. Then fix the board to the vertical battens at 150mm (6in) intervals, working upwards and downwards from the centre. Finally secure the other edges at 100mm (4in) intervals, 12mm ($\frac{1}{2}$in) in from the edge.

Finishing off For an attractive finish you can use either emulsion paint or wallpaper. Before painting, use glasspaper to round off the board edges and key the surface for the paint. Prime the boards with special hardboard primer or diluted emulsion paint (one part water to four parts paint) before giving the finishing coats. If using wallpaper, first seal the boards with a coat of hardboard primer.

Insulating ceilings

In the average house most heat is lost through the roof and it has been estimated that more than a quarter of the homes in Britain have either no lofts or no access to loft space. In such cases insulating the underside of the upstairs ceiling is the only effective answer. Fixing 13mm ($\frac{1}{2}$in) fibre insulating board tiles to the ceiling will reduce the heat loss from the house in winter by about ten per cent; the time it takes to heat up a room is also reduced. Using decorated tiles ensures an attractive finish. from the house in winter by about ten per cent; the

Planning and fixing

First decide on the method of fixing. If the ceiling can be easily cleaned and is reasonably flat, fixing the tiles direct to the ceiling with acoustic tile adhesive is the easiest and most economical way. If the ceiling is loose, badly cracked or very uneven, it will be necessary to screw wood battens through the ceiling to the timbers above.

Measure the ceiling and other surfaces to be tiled. For a symmetrical job, with equal margins of cut tiles at opposite sides of the room, it is worthwhile drawing the areas to be tiled on a planning grid. This will not only act as a guide to the number of tiles required but will also help in determining the positions, lengths and number of battens, if these are to be used, and amount of adhesive needed.

Insulating board tiles usually come in 305 × 305mm (12 × 12in) sizes in cartons of 30, 60 or 100. Adhesive manufacturers also normally state the covering capacity of their products – for example, 1 litre for 2sq m (or 2pt for 22sq ft) of tile area.

Direct gluing First wash down the ceiling with household detergent or a solution of water and sugar soap and scrape away any stubborn flaking paint. Check the corners are square by drawing a line at right-angles to the longer wall. Plan to start fixing in a corner with the first row of tiles against the longer wall.

With a putty knife apply 25mm (1in) diameter blobs of acoustic tile adhesive to the back of the tiles at each corner. Press the tiles into place on the ceiling, ensuring each tile lines up with the one before. Adhesive can be applied to a number of tiles at a time and the tiles fixed one after the other.

Tiles which fit together with tongues and grooves

Fixing tongued and grooved tiles

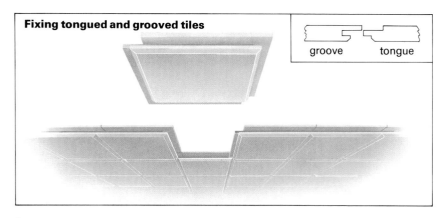

groove   tongue

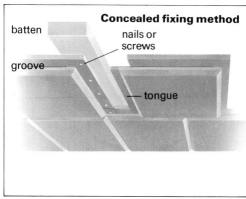

Concealed fixing method

batten

nails or screws

groove

tongue

Fixing to battens (ceiling)

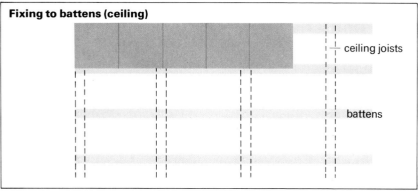

ceiling joists

battens

Section of finished surface

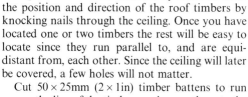

ceiling joists

ceiling

gap

batten

cove

tiles

are easier to use and give a more level finish. For the first row, however, remember to cut off one of the tongues on each tile so the plain edges go next to the wall, allowing a small gap for expansion.

Fixing to battens First establish by trial and error the position and direction of the roof timbers by knocking nails through the ceiling. Once you have located one or two timbers the rest will be easy to locate since they run parallel to, and are equidistant from, each other. Since the ceiling will later be covered, a few holes will not matter.

Cut 50×25mm (2×1in) timber battens to run across the line of the timbers and screw them to the timbers at 305mm (12in) intervals. Make sure the undersides of the battens are level with one another, packing them if necessary with offcuts of hardboard.

Fix the tiles to the battens with staples or round head nails. With tongued and grooved tiles the fixings are concealed by the tongue of the next tile.

Finishing For the best finish fix cove to cover the join between the tiles and the walls.

Insulating floors

Standard hardboards are used to improve both timber and concrete floors. On suspended timber floors you can eliminate draughts and so reduce heat loss by nailing hardboard to the floor, making sure the joins in the hardboard and the floor do not coincide. Hardboard applied to plain-edged floorboards above lath and plaster ceilings provides the minimum fire resistance required by current building regulations. Again, the joins in the hardboard and the floor must not coincide.

Heat insulation on concrete floors is improved by bonding sheets of insulation board in place with bituminous adhesive. Cover this with carpeting or, if you intend to place heavy items on the floor, use a harder-surfaced insulating board.

Never put down hardboard or insulating board on a concrete floor where damp is suspected. Treatment for this situation has already been described – see page 62 onwards.

Insulating doors

You can improve the fire resistance of old panelled doors by fixing on hardboard. To do this you will have to remove the door and take off the fitments. Glue medium board into the existing panels and cover the whole door with 3mm ($\frac{1}{8}$in) standard hardboard, nailed into place. The extra thickness of hardboard on the door may mean you have to re-hang the door further away from the closure bead (by extending the hinge recesses in the door frame) or move the closure bead further away.

Order of nailing hardboard to floorboards

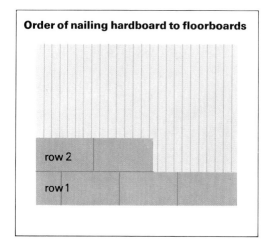

row 2

row 1

Fixing hardboard to panelled door

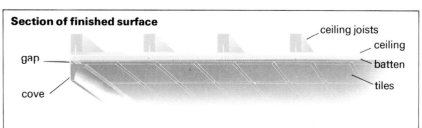

panels filled with hardboard   hardboard covering

Coping with condensation

For most people condensation conjures up pictures of bathroom walls running with moisture, windows steamed up and water on the window sills. These more easily recognizable forms of condensation can be temporarily cleared up with a little time and effort devoted to mopping up. But there are ways of helping to prevent condensation forming in the first place.

Condensation is caused when moisture in warm air comes into contact with a cold surface and turns to water. Kitchens and bathrooms are the obvious places to suffer, but condensation will often occur in patches on walls or ceilings in living areas too.

Windows

Single glass windows are undoubtedly one of the worst offenders in causing condensation. In damp winter conditions few homes escape the problem – and bedrooms in particular suffer from its effects. This is the result of lower night temperatures reacting with the warm air we breathe out or warm air circulated by heating equipment.

The problem is made worse by the introduction of new moist air into a room by cooking, using hand basins or running baths. Probably the worst effect of condensation is the damage it can do in a short time to window frames and paintwork. Even when frames are correctly painted 3mm ($\frac{1}{8}$in) in on the glass pane, the lower beading quickly breaks down

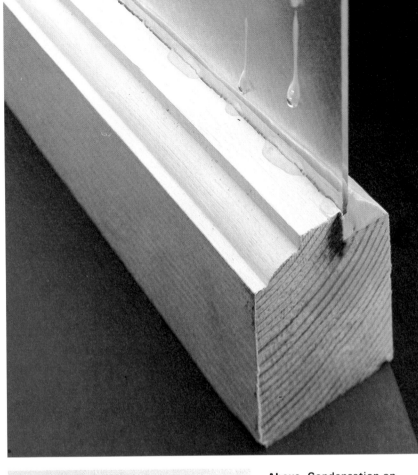

Above Condensation on window will break down paint surface and attack wood or metal frame

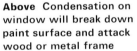

Far left When lining walls with expanded polystyrene, hang first length and over-lap second length by about 13mm ($\frac{1}{2}$in). Check with your supplier on suitable adhesive
Left Trim halfway across overlap through both thicknesses of polystyrene

Far left Peel away both trimmed edges
Left Stick back edges, having applied more adhesive to wall, to give flush finish to join

To test for damp floor, place piece of glass on ring of Plasticine over affected area
Right Moisture on underside of glass indicates penetrating damp
Below right Moisture forming on top of glass indicates condensation present

and allows moisture to attack the timber or metal beneath.

One remedy is the installation of good quality double-glazing. Although condensation may not be completely eliminated, the build-up is reduced sufficiently to prevent moisture being a problem.

Bathrooms

Decorative materials with cold surfaces, such as ceramic tiles, are renowned for the rapid formation of condensation. The build-up can be quickly dispersed by opening the windows. An extractor fan set into the window or mounted on (or ducted to) an exterior wall will also help remove vapour quickly. You can reduce condensation in cold bathrooms by heating the room for a short time before running the bath water. But remember you must use wall or ceiling-mounted heaters of the type recommended for bathrooms. Try running a little cold water into the bath before you turn on the hot tap, as this will also help reduce condensation.

Other wall surfaces

The real problem areas are patches of condensation which sometimes appear in odd corners of the home. Often these go unnoticed until a patch of mould appears. Poor circulation of air is one of the prime causes and on a damp day a short burst of warm air from a fan heater, or a hair dryer, will help to check condensation.

If mould persists – and the surface is not wallpapered – rinse the wall with a strong solution of bleach. If the surface is wallpapered you will have to remove the paper and line the wall with rolls of expanded polystyrene which you can then wallpaper over or paint with emulsion. In severe cases this may not be completely successful and a painted wall, which can be treated with bleach from time to time, is preferable.

Penetrating damp

Patchy wall condensation is often confused with penetrating damp. Removal of a small area of plaster should tell you which it is. If it is condensation, the brick area behind will be perfectly dry; if it is damp, try to find the cause. At ground floor level it could be a faulty damp proof course; upstairs it may be a faulty gutter or down pipe or driving rain on porous solid brickwork might be the reason. Try to increase the circulation by warm, dry air in the affected area, but remedy the cause of the problem as soon as possible otherwise the trouble will recur.

Ceilings

Those with a high gloss finish are most susceptible to condensation and covering the area with expanded polystyrene, cork or fibre tiles will help solve the problem.

Damp floors

These are often caused by damp from the outside and not by condensation. You can make a simple test to see which condition is present with a piece of glass on a ring of Plasticine, as shown above.

Condensation on floors usually occurs with cold-surfaced materials on concrete, such as tiles in the kitchen. The most effective remedy is to substitute cork or a similar warm-surfaced flooring.

Double glazing

While heat losses vary depending on the nature of a building and its aspect, in a typical uninsulated house about 15 percent of house heat is lost through the windows. If all the windows in such a house are double-glazed, this heat loss will be halved to give a seven and a half percent saving on fuel bills. There are many factors which can affect this figure – for example, the type of system used and how well it is fitted. Installing double glazing in an old cottage with just a few small windows would not obtain this saving, whereas there will be higher savings in a modern 'goldfish bowl' type of property.

Double glazing is not a money saver on the scale of other forms of insulation such as glass fibre laid in the loft or cavity wall infill; however, there are a number of reasons why you will find the necessary expenditure worthwhile to add to the comfort of your home. An efficient system will eliminate cold, draughty areas round windows, making the whole floor area of a room usable on cold days, and rooms will seem larger without the need for occupants to cluster round the fire or radiators.

Preventing condensation

When rooms are properly heated and ventilated, condensation will be reduced and possibly eliminated by double-glazed windows, since the inner panes of glass will be warmer and less susceptible to misting. With some double glazing systems, interpane misting may occur; this is usually slight and can be wiped away provided the new window is hinged or sliding. Alternatively you can place silica gel crystals between the panes of glass; these absorb moisture and, when saturated, should be temporarily removed and dried in a warm oven.

Misting on the room side of the window indicates the temperature of the glass is too low, given the water content of the room's atmosphere; by a process of trial and error, you should carry out adjustment until there is a proper balance between heat and ventilation in the room.

Condensation on the cavity surface of the outer glass is usually a sign that moist air is leaking into the cavity from the room. Make the seal round the new double glazing as airtight as possible, using a

1 Sachets of silica gel crystals placed between the two panes of glass can help reduce interpane misting; when saturated, the sachets should be removed, dried in a warm oven and replaced
2 To cure condensation on the cavity surface of the outer glass, drill ventilation holes right through the primary frame
3 Drill the ventilation holes 10mm deep and pack them with glass fibre to act as a filter

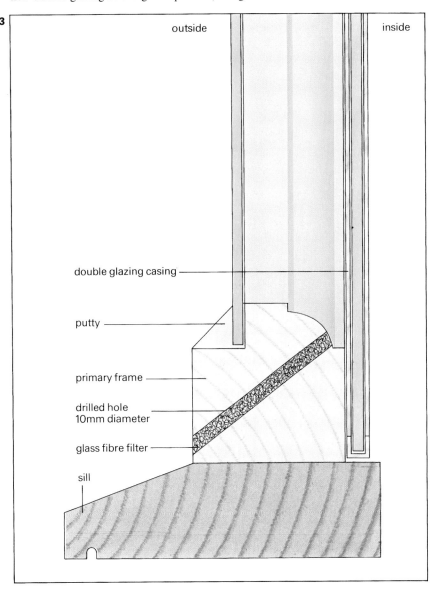

outside   inside

double glazing casing

putty

primary frame

drilled hole 10mm diameter

glass fibre filter

sill

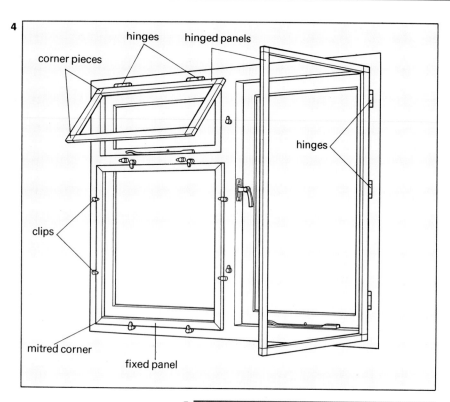

4 Installing fixed or hinged double glazing. The new panes are fitted in aluminium or plastic U-shaped channel, joined at the corners by mitring or by using special corner pieces; use hinges to fix the panels to opening windows and clips for fixed windows

5 Using plastic film as double glazing; cut the film to size and fix it to the frame with double-sided adhesive tape

tape form of draught excluder, and seal any gaps in the joints of a timber framework with a matching wood filler, making sure the filler penetrates through to the full depth of the joint.

If this fails to cure the problem, drill ventilation holes through the primary frame to the drier air outside. In a 1m (39in) wide window, two 10mm (or ⅜in) diameter holes set 500mm (or 20in) apart should be sufficient. More will be needed for larger windows; you can decide the exact number by a process of trial and error – drilling an extra hole and waiting to see if this cures the problem. Pack the holes with glass fibre to act as an air filter.

With hermetically sealed units (see below) the air in the cavity is dried, so condensation between the panes is not possible as long as the seals remain sound; failure of the seals is a rare occurrence, but reputable manufacturers give long-term guarantees to cover the possibility.

Sound insulation
Installing a good quality double glazing system will give a substantial reduction in the decibel level of noise permeating through windows from typical town traffic or a local playground. However, if your noise problem is more acute, noise prevention is a more extensive technical matter – the actual source of the noise, the location of the house, the type of glass thickness needed, the distance the two panes are set apart and any additional insulation around windows or between the double glazing should all be considered before you buy any expensive system to solve the problem.

Remember Government grants to install double glazing can be given to people living in certain heavy traffic areas or where there is an airport nearby. Your local authority will be able to supply details and advice.

In normal noise level situations the two sheets of glass in a double glazing system should be at least 100mm (or 4in) apart to provide adequate sound insulation. To provide effective thermal insulation, the optimum gap should be of 19mm (¾in). If you want both sound and thermal insulation, you should select a wider gap of up to 200mm (or 8in); you will find thermal insulation is not greatly reduced in this case.

Buying double glazing

Certain double glazing firms do not cater for the DIY market, others cater for both professional and DIY work and some solely for the DIY market. If you choose a professional installation, a representative from the company will call on you, discuss your requirements, measure up and arrange for the work to be carried out by company operatives. If you choose to install double glazing yourself, you will find local retail outlets stock at least one kind of kit for the framework. Measure up your requirements and buy the correct size; then read the instructions carefully to find out the thickness of glass required – 3 or 4mm (or ⅛ or ⅙ in) – and the height and width of glass. Glass can vary in price, so it is well worth shopping around.

One or two companies offer a mail order service whereby you measure up, send the firm the dimensions and they return a kit – in one case at least the glass also is supplied. At least one company offers the best of both worlds – a company representative will call and measure up and you will then receive a tailor-made kit complete with glass. The advantage of this method of buying double glazing is the company takes responsibility for any errors in measuring and making the framework; also, since you are dealing directly with a company and not through a middle man, this system is often less expensive than other systems.

Costs Depending on the house style and the system chosen, to double glaze all the windows in a house could be a costly business. You could reduce the amount by completing only selected windows – perhaps those in the living room, hall and landing or a particularly draughty bedroom. A little-used dining room or spare bedroom might not be worth the expense; it would probably be better to keep the doors of these rooms closed and well sealed in cold weather to prevent the house heat drifting into them. When they are in use, heavy curtains pulled across would be as effective as double glazing, as long as the windows have been effectively draught-proofed.

Factors which can drastically affect the price of double glazing one window, let alone all the windows in the house, are obviously the cost of the glass and the retail price of the kit you choose, which again can differ from shop to shop.

Types of double glazing
There are four types of double glazing in common use: insulating glass, secondary sashes, coupled windows and plastic film.

Insulating (hermetically sealed) glass These units look like a single pane of glass and consist of two pieces of glass joined together and hermetically sealed in the factory – a process in which the air space between the panes is dried to prevent misting when installed. The pieces of glass are sealed with edge spacers of metal, alloy or plastic. The units are tailor-made and replace a single pane, enabling a window to open and close normally.

There are two types – standard and stepped. The stepped units are ideal where there are shallow rebates since installation can be carried out without having to alter the existing frame to accept the new units. The existing frame must be well fitting and sound enough to take the extra weight which will be imposed by the units.

Secondary sashes This is the most popular DIY method of installing double glazing. A second pane of glass in its own frame is secured to the existing frame or to the inner or outer sill and reveal; in some circumstances it is possible to fit the new window outside the existing frame. The existing window remains unaltered to form the other half of the double glazing. Manufacturers supply frames of aluminium or plastic; other types consist of plastic extrusions which are cut to length and joined with corner fittings to enable a frame for the glass to be made up. Hinges or clips are then used to secure the secondary sash to the existing window. The secondary sash is movable for cleaning, ventilation or summer storage and can be fixed, hinged or sliding.

Coupled windows These are usually specified only for new buildings or where entire frames are being replaced during conversion. One single-glazed window has an auxiliary window coupled to it, allowing both to move together. They are fitted with hinges and fasteners so the frames can be separated for cleaning purposes.

Plastic film This is a low-cost one-season option which can be a very effective form of double glazing for fixed windows. Plastic film is cut to size and applied to the window frame with double-sided adhesive tape. If you use this method, make sure that where windows are to be opened they are double-glazed separately from fixed panes; if a complete film was stretched across the entire window it would not be possible to open the window without first removing the film.

If you are restricted to a very small budget, you can use kitchen self-clinging plastic to make a form of double glazing for small panes. For larger panes, you will have to break up the pane space with a thin timber framework to create the effect of smaller panes and fix the film inside these smaller areas.

Installing double glazing
If you are going to install your own double glazing, it is likely you will choose a secondary sash type since kits for these are widely available and are relatively easy to install.

There are, however, a number of problems you may come across when fitting them. For example,

they can be fitted to existing timber or metal window frames; but if metal frames are fixed directly into masonry, you will have to drill and tap the frame to provide screw-fixing points or fit a secondary timber frame to accept the double glazing, particularly if the frame is too narrow. However, most metal windows are set in a timber surround and this can be treated as the window.

If you want to fix the double glazing frame to the reveal, you may come across the problem of an out-of-square reveal; to deal with this you will have to pack the out-of-square area with timber wedges or choose a system which fits directly to the window. Again, certain types of kit require the channels in which the new glazing is fitted to be mitred at the corners and joined. If you think you will find this too much of a problem, choose a type which is supplied with corner pieces. Remember to cut the channel lengths squarely at the ends or you will find it difficult to fit on the corner pieces and the final appearance of the glazing will be marred. Also, don't expect the glass to be a push-fit into the channel; it might slide in, but often you will need to encourage this by tapping gently with a mallet or with a hammer and a block of wood placed to protect the glass.

Warning If you are going to double glaze bay windows, remember to treat each window as a separate unit.

There are many makes of secondary sash double glazing available and the manufacturers supply

6 Fitting sliding secondary sashes; this type may be fixed to the face of the window or to the reveal
7 Fitting shatterproof panels into self-adhesive plastic track; mark the sill trim where it reaches the edge of the frame
8 Cut the side channel to length, remove the adhesive backing and press the strip onto the wall
9 Fit the top channel along the top of the frame
10 To shape the panels, score with a sharp knife and break over the edge of a firm surface
11 Fit the first panel, slit the top channel at the end of the panel and clip in place
12 Fix a panel divider and continue fitting the panels
13 Fit the final panel, ensuring the side channel is pressed firmly along its length
14 The finished installation; separate panels can be removed by opening the channel at the top and side

6

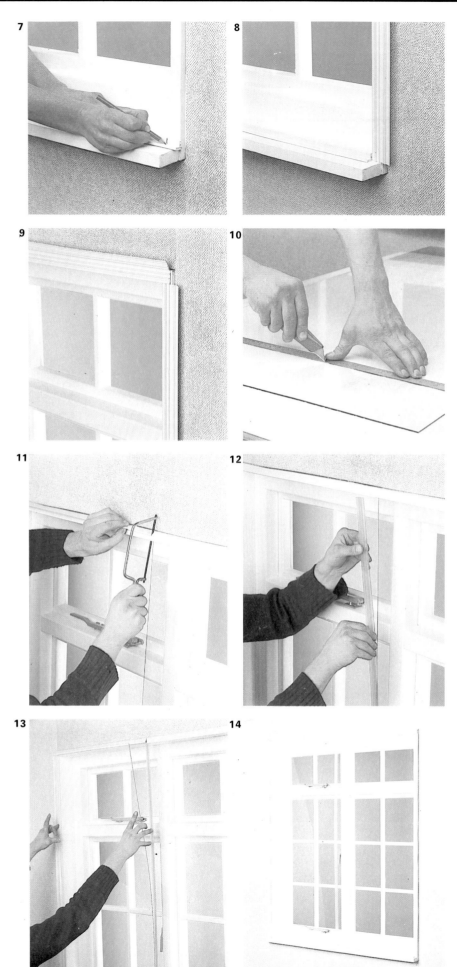

detailed instructions for installation. There are, however, three basic types of system: plastic channel, fixed or hinged, and sliding secondary sashes.

Plastic channel With this type, each pane of glass is fitted into a frame made by cutting lengths of U-shaped plastic channel to size; remove any sharp edges from the glass with a carborundum stone. The corners of the channel have to be mitred. Using a sharp knife and a mitre guide, cut the first mitre corner and then fit the channel to the glass to determine the position of the second corner. Remove the channel and mitre-cut at this position; repeat this process until all four corners have been cut. Secure the channel to the glass; some kits require the use of adhesive to form a rigid frame. Hold this assembly up to the window and fix it in place on the frame with the plastic clips supplied with the kit.

With this type of double glazing, out-of-square reveals will not cause problems since the channel is always fixed to the frame.

Fixed or hinged Usually this type consists of plastic or aluminium channel cut to shape and joined at the corners by mitring or by using special corner pieces. Fixing is either by clips to non-opening windows or by hinges to opening windows (the new windows can be hinged to open sideways or upwards). You could, of course, use hinges with fixed windows to make them easier to clean. This type of double glazing will, if correctly assembled, eliminate draughts and the new windows can be removed for summer storage.

Before you buy this type of system, read the manufacturer's instructions carefully to check the frame around your window is wide enough to take the double glazing and that it is made of the right material to take this particular system. With some systems the manufacturer recommends fixing only to wood rather than metal frames. Again, your existing window catches or handles may protrude in such a way they will interfere with the installation of the new system. You can usually solve these problems by fitting a secondary timber frame to take the double glazing; butt-join the corners of the frame, fill in any gaps with wood filler and apply a wood primer followed by two coats of paint, allowing the first coat to dry before applying the second.

There is one system which uses PVC shatterproof panels instead of glass. These are fitted into self-adhesive plastic tracks which are cut and pressed into place to the wall outside the reveal. The panels can be easily removed, but you may consider this too much trouble with opening windows.

Sliding Usually this type is fitted in the reveal. An outer frame is fixed in the reveal to square up the opening; use pieces of wood as packing if necessary. The glass is fixed in a separate frame which is fitted inside the outer frame to enable the glass and its separate frame to slide. The framed glass is removable and horizontal and vertical sliders are available. Depending on the size of the window, two or more sliding panels will be needed.

One system can be fixed to the face of the window frame so you will avoid the problems of squaring up a reveal, although it can be reveal-fixed as well. In this case the company offers a kit specially designed to suit your windows; it comprises plastic channelling cut to size and ready to be joined on site so no cutting or mitring is required. The glass comes complete in its tailor-made frame ready to be installed in the channelling.